Advance Praise for

PRACTICE WHAT YOU PREACH

"With compelling evidence, Maister blows away the mysteries as to what makes a high performance team. He offers great insights and definitive actions."
—Michael Albrecht, Jr., Global Executive, IBM

"Required reading for any serious manager of a professional services organization."
—Mel Bergstein, CEO, DiamondCluster International

"Offers validation and healthy discomfort as we consider what running an excellent professional business is all about."
—Roger Brossy, Managing Director, Nextera/Sibson Consulting Group

"An absolute must read for any manager who is serious about achieving the elusive goal of creating a high achievement culture. A rare blend of important practical advice and sound, accessible scholarship."
—Richard B. Chase, Justin Dart Professor of Operations Management, University of Southern California

"Excellent. Finally, clear proof that attracting, retaining, motivating, and exciting people is the key strategy for financial success."
—Tony D'Aloisio, Chief Executive Partner, Mallesons Stephen Jaques, Australia

"Reconfirms his commitment to enhance professional service firms by emphasizing the importance of paying attention to the human assets."
—Professor Thomas DeLong, Harvard Business School

"Provides concrete proof that financial success comes from hiring good people, energizing them, and turning them loose! Also tells you precisely how to do it."
—Paul Dunn, Chairman, Results Accountants' Systems

"A must for leaders who want to make their firms not only more financially successful but, more important, much better for their clients and their people."
—Claudio Fernández-Aráoz, Executive Committee, Egon Zehnder International

"Maister has done it again—yet another insight-filled book that will facilitate your growth as a business leader and manager."
—**Robert R. Garland, National Managing Partner of Assurance and Advisory Services, Deloitte & Touche**

"Shows what it takes to lead the truly successful professional service firm. Courage and commitment with a strong dose of common sense are the glue that brings it all together."
—**Richard E. Izard, CA, President, Thurber Engineering Ltd., Canada**

"Well researched, insightful, and with practical advice relevant to all leaders and managers . . . will challenge the thinking, courage and conviction of leaders around the globe."
—**Paul Koenig, National Managing Partner, Tax and Legal Services, PricewaterhouseCoopers Australia**

"This is a straight-talking, data-based, and energy-infused work of uncompromising scholarship and incomparable practicality. You will find tough-minded, hard-nosed, yet compassionate lessons from the solid research of the person universally regarded as the professional's professional. There is absolutely nothing else like this book on the shelves, and you must have it on yours."
—**James M. Kouzes, coauthor of *The Leadership Challenge* and of *Credibility,* and Chairman Emeritus, Tom Peters Company**

"Proves that the most successful professional service firms are those that are doing more than just chasing money. . . . A compelling argument for values-based management."
—**Linda Listrom, Executive Committee, Jenner & Block**

"Provides hard evidence on management issues that are often neglected because they are perceived to be intangible. This book makes them tangible—and shows them to be critical to success."
—**Robert Millard, Director, Environmental Impact Management Services (Pty) Ltd., South Africa**

"A detailed empirical study . . . essential reading for all leaders of professional service firms."
—**Professor Adrian Payne, Cranfield University School of Management**

"Clearly demonstrates that if managers treat their people as their first priority, the people will more likely create and take very good care of grateful clients."
—Ronald D. Peyton, President and CEO, Callan Associates Inc.

"Confirms the acuteness of Maister's analysis and the quality of his management teaching. He is indisputably one of today's greatest management teachers for professional firms."
—Jean-Jacques Raquin, Managing Partner, Gide Loyrette Nouel, France

"Maister has been a guiding light for professional firms for many years. . . . This book goes to the heart of all management issues by addressing the need to develop people and treat them like gold."
—Dean McMann, CEO, Ransford

"Nice guys don't finish last; they build winning professional teams. If you seek to build an extraordinary client service culture, read this book!"
—Stuart Scott, Chairman and Chief Executive Officer, Jones Lang LaSalle

"Reveals the true sources of profitability, relevant to corporations as well as professional firms. Chapter 9 alone will change how you manage and will increase your profitability."
—Adrian Slywotzky, Co-author, "How Digital Is Your Business?" "The Profit Zone," and "Value Migration"

"Reassures all who value integrity, trust, and respect for employees. Punchy and practical, the message is refreshing and universally applicable."
—Professor Richard Susskind, author of *The Future of Law* and *Transforming the Law*

"Extremely readable. . . . Offers help and hope to the managers of all professional service firms, and should be kept no more than an arm's length away from every managing partner's desk."
—Dick Tyler, Managing Partner, CMS Cameron McKenna

"Destined to be a classic. Provides empirical evidence of what drives success for employees, clients, and shareholders. We practice these principles, and benefit greatly from them."
—Tom Watson, Vice Chairman & Chief Growth Officer, Omnicom Group Inc.

"A great 'how to succeed' manual for organizations in any field. Maister confirms that success is not about programs and policies, but is about the honesty, integrity, and courage of the leader."
   —Lawrence A. Weinbach, Chairman and CEO, Unisys Corporation

"Full of powerful 'home truths' supported by conclusive evidence that taking care of employees' needs is very good business, indeed."
   —William N. Weld, Director, Aon University

"This sequel to *The Trusted Advisor* could just as easily have been named *The Trusted Employer*. Maister demonstrates that leaders who walk the talk really do create more successful businesses."
   —Tony Williams, Managing Partner, Andersen Legal

"Obligatory reading for managers. Solid data and case studies make the messages come alive."
   —Vicky Wright, Group Managing Director, Hay Group

PRACTICE

What Managers Must Do

WHAT YOU

to Create a High Achievement Culture

PREACH

David H. Maister

THE FREE PRESS   New York London Toronto Sydney Singapore

*f*P

THE FREE PRESS
A Division of Simon & Schuster, Inc.
1230 Avenue of the Americas
New York, NY 10020

THE FREE PRESS and colophon are trademarks
of Simon & Schuster, Inc.

Manufactured in the United States of America

10 9 8 7 6 5 4 3 2 1

Library of Congress Cataloging-in-Publication Data Is Available

ISBN 0-7432-1187-1

To Kathy, always and forever

Contents

PRACTICE WHAT YOU PREACH

Introduction

Together with many consultants and authors, I have long argued that if you (first) energize and excite your people, they will serve your clients well, and you'll (then) make lots of money. But is there any actual proof that this is the right sequence?

There is some. *The Service Profit Chain* by Heskett, Sasser and Schlesinger argues the case for this model convincingly. Kotter and Heskett, in *Corporate Culture and Performance* investigated the relationship between culture and profitability. In *First, Break All the Rules,* Buckingham and Coffman reported on the behaviors of successful managers in a way that supports the core proposition. In *Built to Last,* Collins and Porras described the characteristics of successful industrial corporations in detail and arrived at similar conclusions.

I present in this book the results of a study that assembles data and evidence on the factors that drive financial success. Surveying 139 offices of 29 firms in 15 countries in 15 different lines of business, I asked a simple question: are employee attitudes correlated with financial success?

The answer, as this book will show, is an unequivocal "yes!" The most financially successful businesses do better than the rest on virtually every aspect of employee attitudes, and those that do best on employee attitudes are measurably more profitable. What is even more powerful, as the book shows, it is attitudes that drive financial results, and not (predominantly) the other way round.

None of this should be taken to mean that client service, client relations and quality are not crucial. As we shall see, they are. Conventional wisdom is right in saying that quality and great client service gets results. (We will provide proof of that, too.) However, what conventional wisdom forgets is that great client service is itself a product of other things. To get great client service, it turns out, you must first energize your people to deliver it. And that brings us to what may be the prime mover of this entire chain of effects: the skills and behavior of the manager in creating and driving everything else.

Of all the goals that businesses say they have (make money, please clients, attract and develop talented staff), the least well done are those related to managing people. Yet not only are people a key link in the chain of activities that create profits, but we are also living through a war for talent—a people crisis—where every business is short of people. To be weak in this area (as so many firms are) is akin to shooting yourself in the foot.

The study produces very specific (and nontrivial) findings. We shall see that the most financially successful operations share a number of characteristics:

- ❏ Management is seen as operating in accordance with the firm's overall philosophy and values. They practice what they preach, and there are no disconnects between the walk and the talk.
- ❏ Management is trusted by those they manage. Individual managers act in the interests of their group, not just to advance the manager's personal interests.
- ❏ People's personal potential is being fulfilled and realized, according to the people being managed.
- ❏ There is a high degree of loyalty and commitment, again driven by individual managers.
- ❏ Compensation systems are equitably managed.
- ❏ Firms do not compromise their standards in hiring simply to meet a capacity need. People quality is seen as high.

The evidence shows that these are high standards that few managers (or management teams) reach consistently. They are not easy to achieve. They require courage, an ability to confront difficult situations, and an ability to take a long-term perspective when many pressures cry out for much earlier gratification.

The standards are not commonly achieved, but when they are, we can now show that they *cause* (yes, cause) a demonstrable, measurable improvement in financial performance (including growth rates as well as profits).

The standards are tough. They do not say, gently, "we encourage teamwork." They say things like "we have no room" for individualists. The message is that management must have the guts and courage to enforce the standards they frequently preach.

The list of key profit drivers revealed here represents a balanced package. There is no one secret to success. We shall see that you have to do well on a combination of client relationships, compensation system fairness, skill building, and other factors. Robert Kaplan and David Norton wrote a wonderful book, *The Balanced Scorecard,* about the importance of paying attention to a well-chosen mix of performance areas. This book can tell you precisely what that balanced scorecard needs to be.

Most of the findings confirm what other writers (and I) have been advocating for years. What's new here is that this study presents substantial evidence.

Some of the conclusions *are* new. Among the top factors predicting profitability are the issues of trust and respect. These were not introduced by my personal theories. They were the result of cold statistical analysis. The study shows that where trust and respect between management and employees are high, financial performance predictably goes up.

Surprising? Maybe. But we are rarely (if ever) taught how to win, earn, or give trust and respect in our formal education. This book will show you how. It reaffirms the importance of personal character in leading a firm to greatness.

On a related point, the book shows that success in management is less a property of firms (the systems of the business as a whole) but, instead, is mostly about the personality of the individual manager within the operating unit. Success is about personalities, not policies.

In spite of presenting extensive data and statistical analysis, the core of the book is not the numbers. It is the interviews, anecdotes, stories and personal experiences of the managers who got the best results in this survey. I report on who the paragons are that were able to achieve truly stellar financial results, while also energizing, enthusing and exciting their staff. What, precisely, do they do?

Although they asked to remain anonymous (a condition of doing the research), these superstar managers gave permission to reveal their concrete secrets. The findings will challenge you. How well, it will ask, do you pass the tests of trust, respect and integrity? Are you seen as practicing what you preach? I will show that if you *can't* pass these tests, you *will* make less money!

The Database

The data used in this book come from a survey of 139 offices in 29 firms owned by the same publicly held marketing communications company. Sixty-eight percent of the offices were in the United States, and 32 percent were in other countries, including Belgium, Brazil, Canada, China, England, France, Germany, Hong Kong, Ireland, Italy, Japan, Mexico, Netherlands, Scotland and Spain.

The businesses covered in this study include advertising, public relations, brand identity consulting, health-care consulting, direct mail, Internet (web) marketing, promotion, public affairs consulting, employee communications and many others.

All the firms have significant autonomy. Each of the firms (indeed, each of the offices) is free to choose its own management style and approach, thus allowing us to examine the implications of differing office cultures and management styles.

The range of firm sizes was from one office to twenty-four offices. The individual offices ranged in size from 10 to 351 employees. The average number of employees in any given office was 43.

The word "employee" in this survey covered everyone working in the firm, from top to bottom, from top managers to mailroom clerks. No distinction was made between partners and nonpartners, owners and employees, managers and staff. Similarly, employees in all roles were surveyed, including both fee-earning staff and those in support roles.

There were a total of 5,589 individual respondents (a 55 percent response rate), after eliminating offices with fewer than ten people and all employees earning less than U.S.$25,000 per year.

How Does All This Apply to You?

If you are not in the marketing communications business, I suspect that, throughout this book, you will ask yourself, "Does any or all of this apply to me?"

Let's start with the obvious: This study does not include accounting, law, architecture, financial services, executive search, engineering or a host of other businesses and professions. So, we don't have *direct* data here for those (or many other) businesses.

On the other hand, we do have a great deal of diversity here. We have businesses ranging from premium-fee consulting operations to low-fee, high-volume execution-intensive businesses. We have businesses with immensely high leverage and those staffed almost entirely with senior-level counselors. We have businesses that deal only with the client's executive suite, and others that have to work through purchasing directors.

Some of these businesses have ongoing relationships that last for decades, while others have to compete every time for every individual project. Some are large, global operations while still others are tiny, regional operations working far from major financial centers or other big cities. And many national differences are covered in the database.

As a result of all this diversity, any lessons we can glean that seem to apply across all these businesses have a good chance of being lessons that should be taken seriously by businesses not explicitly included here. That's my hypothesis, but you be the judge.

How to Use This Book

The book is written for the practicing manager. I have tried to write the text in plain language, and defer all statistical language and presentation to the appendices. Those who wish to investigate the supporting data in depth can look there. However, if you choose, you should be able to read straight through the book without referring to the appendices.

Whatever contribution this book makes lies less in innovative conclusions than in the fact that I have tried to present new *evidence* to support important, but perhaps familiar, conclusions. (Hence the book's title: the message is not to preach new things, but to practice what most managers and firms already preach.)

Accordingly, the book is built around the evidence, quantitative and anecdotal, that I obtained. It unfolds slowly, presenting the results of analyses one at a time, building up from the simplest to the most complex. Similarly, rather than open the book with the major lessons learned from the case studies as a whole, I invite you to read each of the case studies one at a time, and experience them as I did, with (I hope) growing cumulative impact. The summary is deferred until the latter portion of the book.

For those who *do* wish to get the book's main conclusions right away, there's a relatively simple way to do it. Skim chapter 1 then jump straight to chapter 7 (The Predictive Package); chapter 9 (The Path to Performance); and Chapters 20 to 23 (Lessons). These chapters summarize the most important statistical and case study evidence in the their most essential form.

However, the story is richer than those chapters alone, and I hope that most readers will come with me as I recreate the journey of discovery that this research took me on.

Keep an eye out for lessons in the evidence that I may have failed to stress! While I will provide summaries and tell you what I think the lessons of the evidence are, you may want to keep a yellow highlighter pen handy to mark the lessons *you* deem to be the most important.

CHAPTER ONE

The Survey

To ensure a comprehensive view, four measures of financial performance were obtained for each of the offices in this study:

- ❏ Two-year percentage growth in revenues
- ❏ Two-year percentage growth in profit
- ❏ Profit margin
- ❏ Profit per employee

These were then combined into a single financial performance score by averaging each office's performance on all four measures, giving equal weight to all four measures, and constructing a financial performance index (Appendix 1). Full financial information was available for 96 offices, compared to the 139 offices that completed the employee survey.

The employee survey was a series of 74 questions with which the respondents were invited to agree or disagree. The full results are shown in Appendix 2.

Seventy-four questions are a lot to examine simultaneously. Fortunately, a technique known as factor analysis allows us to group individual questions into (statistically) related groups or factors.

Applying this technique generated nine groupings or factors (Appendix 3). The nine factors do not include all of the questions, but they are useful as a quick shorthand to look at the results. The nine factors (or question groups) are:

1. Quality and client relationships
2. Training and development
3. Coaching
4. Commitment, enthusiasm and respect
5. High standards
6. Long-term orientation
7. Empowerment
8. Fair compensation
9. Employee satisfaction

The employee responses for each factor are shown in Table 1–1, using the following scale:

6 = Strongly agree; 5 = Agree; 4 = Somewhat agree; 3 = Somewhat disagree; 2 = Disagree; 1 = Strongly disagree

Table 1–1: Scores for Each Factor (Question Group)

Factor (Question Group)	Average Response
Quality and client relationships	4.7
Empowerment	4.7
High standards	4.3
Coaching	4.2
Employee satisfaction	4.2
Long-term orientation	4.0
Commitment, enthusiasm and respect	3.8
Fair compensation	3.7

The message here is clear. The 5,589 respondents in the 139 offices rate quality and client relationships as the area of performance that is currently done best in their office. (Of course, this is what the employees say, not the clients. These results may reflect pride as much as reality.)

They also give high marks for their degree of empowerment, or autonomy (not surprising in a professional environment). It is encouraging to note that they give slightly above average grades to high standards and coaching, although these averages are not high in an absolute sense (4.26, where 4 stands for "somewhat agree.") Employee satisfaction also achieves only modest agreement, overall.

The results for the final four factors are not so encouraging, at least on the surface. Rated lowest of all is training and development. What is immediately apparent is that those things to do with clients are ranked highest, while issues to do with managing people were consistently ranked as being done least well, across offices, across different businesses, across the world.

It is not too surprising that the highest overall average was "only" 4.7. Remember, this is an average across 5,589 individuals in 139 offices. It would take an amazing degree of consensus about true excellence for the *average* of all these people to be much higher. When it comes to the factor groups, we are also averaging across questions, and hence failing to observe some highs and lows.

On the other hand, when the average is as low as 3.5 on a 6-point scale (halfway between somewhat disagree and somewhat agree), as it is for training and development, you can be pretty sure that the few who are doing this well are swamped by the many who are not.

To validate these responses, I asked an additional question in the survey, giving people ten (traditional) goals of a firm and asked them to evaluate how well they thought their individual office was performing on each goal. The scale was from 6 ("We're superb at this") to 1 ("We're very weak at this"). The results are given in Table 1–2.

Table 1–2: Scores on the Ten Goals

Goal	Average (Median)
Quality client service	4.9
Quality of work	4.8
Market reputation	4.7
Long-term client relationships	4.7
Profitability	4.5
Growth	4.3
Being a great place to work	4.0
Innovativeness and creativity	4.0
Collaboration and teamwork	3.9
Skill and career development	3.1

The lesson is the same. Client-related goals are rated highest, while anything to do with managing people falls to the bottom.

It is intriguing that the employees rate profit and growth in the middle of the pack. Most of these companies are actually very profitable, among the highest in their industry, and growing very fast. So why do the staff think their office is doing them only moderately well?

One theory is that when it comes to financial results in business, management's desire is always for "more, more, more." Any financial accomplishment is immediately reset as the minimum benchmark, and people are left with the impression that what they have achieved financially is insufficient. It is thus not surprising that they feel that they are only doing "reasonably" well on these financial things, and hence they award average ratings.

Are you *surprised* by all of these results? I am not. While all companies (in every industry) acknowledge their obligations to their three constituencies of clients, shareholders and employees, employees are almost always the third priority on this list.

I have worked extensively not only in the industries covered by this survey, but also in the professions at large, and these results are very familiar. When it comes to meeting its goals for its people, this group of 139 offices is, in my experience, no worse than its competitors (and perhaps, overall, no better).

There is, of course, a troubling paradox here. Many businesses, including professional firms, have nothing to sell *except* their people. Surely it would be a matter of simple logic (or simple self-preservation) for such firms to excel at energizing their people! But, of course, they don't.

One possible explanation is that many firms *assume* that people will be self-starting and inherently self-motivating, and therefore don't work very hard, if at all, at managing them. If managing means reaching out to energize, challenge, exhort, inspire and enthuse individuals on a real-time basis, then little managing takes place inside most firms.

Instead, what passes for management in these businesses is a system of strict financial controls, with periodic general meetings to listen to the latest inspirational speech and unfold the latest branding slogan or mission statement poster. This represents a combination of tight administration and weak attempts at visionary leadership. Even when done well, neither of these is *managing*.

When there are only people at stake, as in a professional firm, interpersonal skills, social interactions, emotional context and personal psychology all play crucial roles. As Charlie Green (my co-author on *The Trusted Advisor*) points out, people are not just the brains of professional firms, they are the heart, the soul, the guts and the rest of the anatomy as well.

What surprised me, and continues to surprise me, is how many people I meet for whom this is an uncomfortable and, sometimes, unfortunate necessity. Many managers feel most comfortable within the financial, intellectual, rational or artistic boundaries of their field. The realm of dealing with *people* (yeuch!) and *human emotions* (horrors!) is something they feel unprepared for and inclined to avoid whenever they can.

I confess to sometimes feeling this way myself. Wouldn't it be nice if, even occasionally, we could just be purely rational and analytical, without having to deal with the sloppy, messy emotions that interactions with human beings require? Yes, it would be great, but it's not an available option for most of us! And certainly not for those charged with managerial responsibilities.

Further, when selecting people to become managers, firms tend to focus on "business skills" (business development or financial management) rather than people skills. The ability to energize others (i.e., manage) is rarely a primary criterion for choosing managers.

Perhaps the most important questions that follow from this are those that this book is devoted to. Does all this matter? Is it of any consequence that the people-related questions were ranked lowest? Should you care if your office's employees give low marks to the level of commitment, enthusiasm and respect? The answer to all these questions, as this book will show, is: Yes, all of this matters a great deal.

Just so you know what's coming, here's an overview of the quantitative analysis, which I present in steps of increasing statistical rigor.

a) In chapter 3, we look at the most financially successful offices, and see how their scores on the questions differ from all the other offices.

b) In chapter 5, we examine the "correlation coefficients" between each question and the financial performance index, looking to see which employee attitudes tend to

move up and down in synch with the financial index
across the entire range of offices.

c) In chapter 7, we'll look at all the questions simultaneously and analyze which set of questions best predicts
financial performance.

d) Finally, in chapter 9, we'll use an advanced technique to
ask which questions (or question groups) can be said to
cause financial performance.

e) Later quantitative chapters will explore the impact of
office size, age, and line of business on the results.

Interspersed with the quantitative chapters are case studies of the
offices that performed best, both financially and on employee attitudes. We now turn to the first case study, one of the most financially successful offices among all the offices in the database.

CHAPTER TWO

Tramster: A Case Study

Tramster, a marketing consulting firm, achieved a financial performance index more than double that of the study average, increasing its profits twice as fast as the typical office.

It outperformed other offices on many aspects of employee attitudes, from 23 to 47 percent higher than the database average. To get a sense of how much of an increase this is, consider that, across all questions a 7 percent improvement over the average office would put you in the top 25 percent of all offices. So being 23 percent above the average is a lot and 47 percent is huge. (Appendix 4 gives you another way of judging how significant these percentage differences are.)

Here (in descending order) are the ten aspects by which Tramster most exceeded the database average.

1. Enthusiasm and morale around here have never been higher.
2. Considering the office as a whole, the compensation system is managed equitably and fairly.
3. The amount of work I have keeps me challenged, but not overwhelmed.
4. Management around here is trusted.
5. Considering my contribution, I think I am paid fairly compared to others in the office.
6. People within our office always treat others with respect.

7. Management of our office is successful in fostering commitment and loyalty.
8. Communication between the office's management and people at my level is very good.
9. This is a fun place to work.
10. I am highly satisfied with my job.

The CEO (and founder) of Tramster was interviewed to find out how these results were achieved. Also given below are the results of interviews with two groups of mid-level professionals at Tramster. This was done to get their view of things, and to see if what they had to say was consistent with the CEO's view. Let's start with the CEO:

What we are doing to create our financial success is hiring good people, energizing them and turning them loose!

We have also stuck to our niche, our market focus, and we have not diverted from it, even when we had lucrative opportunities to do so. We make it our business to know intimately the plans of all of our most important clients. We are very close to them.

Why are enthusiasm and morale here so high? First of all, we are very profitable and life is good. That certainly helps. But it's not all explained by that. When we started this place my co-founders and I examined what we disliked about the corporate world, and what was nonproductive, and we have eliminated it here.

In big companies you are never told "well done." Here we show appreciation for even small accomplishments, and we do it as soon as the accomplishment happens. We recognize people's successes via a note to the person or announcing it to the group.

We have no special technique or approach for communicating with our people. We just make sure we communicate the things we are thinking and those things that are necessary to help morale and enthusiasm, especially things coming down from our parent company.

To help us with communication (and enthusiasm) issues we decided to put in place an ombudsman system. There are two people who work between upper management and everyone else. One has extensive corporate experience and understands the pulse of communicating both ways. The other, an administrative person who has been with us from the start, is a great liaison.

Their job is to make sure that we in management are aware of and sensitive to what people in the office are concerned about, and to make sure we address these concerns. Having people like this helps because we can read a situation before it has a chance to blossom. Any possible negative situation can be nipped in the bud. Having a lifeline to what is going on is an essential component to the success of the morale issue.

We give people the ability to have a quality of life in addition to their work. There is no seat checking that everyone's here. If someone has a doctor appointment or a PTA meeting the message is "as long as you do your work, just go. Do what you have to do in your life." If you operate this way, people will repay you and come in on off-hours (like a Saturday) when needed.

People say we treat them with respect. It's not very complicated. We don't ask people to do things that we wouldn't do ourselves. We work hard to ensure that management is not viewed as separate and distinct from everyone else. After my corporate experiences, I vowed I would not become detached. All of us, from top to bottom, eat together in the lunchroom at a fixed time. We all brown bag it! It's the best part of day. You get to know your people. No one wants to miss it!

Of course, it's not primarily about the managers. People interact with each other more than they interact with management. People treat *each other* with respect around here; that's the secret. Management's job is to ensure that happens. The biggest reason for this is our teamwork concept. We have always operated on the principle that the best work-product comes from group discussion. We have tried to engender a sense of sharing best practices. We put people together from different disciplines and expertise, thereby encouraging a respect for each other's abilities.

We also manage the level of respect. People in normal life naturally make fun of other people, hopefully in jest. But if I ever hear of anything "nasty" (for example through our ombudsmen) I'll call the person in and let him or her know that insensitive things don't work around here. They are warned. You don't have to do that too often for word to get around.

Would I get rid of such a person if, after counseling, it didn't stop? Even if he or she was a big producer? Yes, without question! But if a person is perceived by everyone as somewhat negative, we do try to emphasize the positives of that person, so employees overall will see them differently. We work hard to give everyone a fair chance. We conduct and believe in diversity and sensitivity training.

We get high trust scores from our people because when we hire them, we are honest about the situation they are entering, including workload, salary, bonus, responsibilities, and everything else. We deliver or exceed on our promises to people (financially) and their job is precisely what we said it was going to be.

Most of our new hires we get from referrals. People come here because other people tell them what it is like to work here. We do an exhaustive review before we bring people in. Trust also comes from the fact that we always do what we say we are going to do. We don't expect people to do what we aren't willing to deliver ourselves. We won't tell people it is a cakewalk when it isn't. The key words are honesty and "we deliver what we say we'll deliver."

Our people say the compensation system is fair. I think this is because we take our performance appraisal system seriously. I personally review with everyone what we make as a firm, what they make and why, and speak with them about their position, so there is lots of open discussion about what is going on with each person.

We also give performance reviews at different times of the year than when we give raises, so that when discussing performance the salary or bonus figure isn't the top thing on the employee's mind. We are paying attention to the actual appraisal. People think it is a fair system and not just a process to deliver money. By speaking with everyone individually, they understand why things are said and done. The personal touch is key.

Numbers do play a part in pay, and raises are based on how the firm does on profitability, how much business a person brings in, and how they handle the business that is given to them to do. But in the end, it's a mix of subjectivity and objectivity. Everyone knows that.

We eliminated nonproductive things like too many meetings. I was sick to death in corporate life with meetings. Meetings here have a *purpose*. We don't ever have a formal process. The only thing formal is the reason we are meeting, which we take very seriously. If an issue is hot, you want to talk about it while you feel hot about it, when the emotion is there. Here everyone is accessible at any time. There are no layers. If our employees want to air something, all they have to do is let that be known.

We have a very low turnover rate, even in these people shortage days. Low turnover saves us a lot of money.

We encourage everyone to be client focused in all ways: work with the client, play golf, entertain, have dinner. The firm will pay. In the corporate world, everything like this has to be approved. Here, people use their own discretion, and do whatever they think is right. We are liberal with expenses necessary to entertain clients, like dinner, golf, and so on. We get tons of business this way.

We also try to bring clients to see our offices. This gives clients a comfort level, like they are a part of us. We always offer them the use of our facilities if they need it, and things like that. Our clients are long term; we give them lots of TLC.

My co-founder's clients know that he would jump off a bridge for them! Everyone else here notices it, admires it and takes their personal cue from his approach. He's a real role model. This is important because it fosters loyalty. It's not a new idea (there *are* few new ideas out there) but different ways of executing always exist.

It is also more fun to work in a group. The client gets a better product and it makes the consultants aware of the fact that "We don't know it all!" Mutual respect here results from working in and thinking in a group.

The thrust here is *not* that we are a happy family. We don't see the need to take things that far. This is a comfortable, friendly place to be, where teamwork is fostered and life outside work is encouraged. There is a difference between working as a team and being a family.

We try to set a good example for our people. We try to use the right language, with no yelling and screaming. People win or lose respect by the way they handle themselves. When I get angry (which is rare), people know why.

If I were giving a lecture, and had to give the secrets to managing a successful business that I didn't know when I started, my advice would be: be a good listener, whether it is to clients, co-workers or subordinates, and be sensitive to people.

I had been told earlier in my life that I was ruthless. That I didn't care about anyone or anything, but just did what I had to do to get the next job done. (I missed everything; my daughter's birthdays, soccer games, and the rest of it. Nothing came before business.) When I started this firm, I knew what a mistake that was, and realized I wanted to be sensitive to the people I worked with and to their lives. It works. The results prove it.

In big companies you have to be successful, but if my corporate employer had a bad year it didn't affect my personal lifestyle. But in a small firm, if you have a big loss, everyone is affected. As the head of the firm, I find myself feeling responsible for maintaining a prosperity level so my people can have prosperous lives. I don't sleep as well now as I did in the big company. I want to make sure my people have a job and are rewarded. I want to give back to people and to community.

You must hire the right people and have the right strategy, and treat clients appropriately. All easy to say, but not always done well. You must make sure you have a good product or service to sell (also often done poorly) and, of course, you can do none of the above without good people.

I would rather have energized people than the cleverness to choose the right niche. Of course, you need to do both. But in the long run, it's better to excel at managing people.

And What Do His People Say?

So that's what the CEO thinks he's doing. To test these comments, let's listen to a group of mid-level people at Tramster. (In this, and our other case studies, I have reported the people's comments as a continuous narrative with no quotation marks. This reporting thus represents a summary of several individual voices combined.). Here's what they had to say:

This organization is small and everyone feels a part of everything. People are involved in multiple projects and with different people. Here you are empowered to do things. On every level you make decisions with the client about activities that are going on. You feel vital to everything. Management gives you the ability to do your own thing, and if they don't agree, you have the right to counter.

People treat each other with respect around here, because everyone's opinion is vital. Input is sought. There is an understanding that all roles are equally important. Everyone eats lunch together every day as a group and everyone knows things about each other's personal lives. We care about things happening in each other's lives and this translates into a working style.

There is no "Do this!" attitude or "I don't want to hear about it." We care about each other. If someone didn't treat others that way, it would be noticed, and they'd be spoken to. Mature attitudes are practiced here.

This is a flat organization. We have no formal reporting structure, no hierarchical reporting systems. This makes for a respectful atmosphere, as does the open-door policy.

The top managers encourage productivity but they know what

everyone's life is all about. When you recognize a person's personal priorities it adds to productivity. People are allowed to run their own projects.

Why is management trusted? They are sensitive to personal issues. They see beyond you as just being a person in the office and what your role here is. I had multiple deaths in my family and a problem with my ex-wife, and management were supportive above and beyond any normal expectation.

This management shares success and failures with everyone. We all worked for weeks on a project proposal. Everyone waited to hear the outcome and when we didn't get the project, the disappointment was shared and personal to everyone. We face successes and failures as a group, as a firm. This creates trust and closeness.

You have to be able to trust each other outside of the personal relationship. You must be able to trust that what everybody around you says they are going to do in relation to work is indeed what they are going to do. You don't have to like someone personally to trust him or her at work. If you're not trustworthy you won't last long here.

There are more opportunities here to move ahead rapidly than at most places, because we are small. Top management encourages you. They ask whether you feel comfortable with your project. They encourage you to take charge of their projects so that they can move onto developing new business.

They encourage you to grow with the job. At all levels you are encouraged to do more and more as time goes on. Everyone grows. Achievement gets recognized. It can happen "on the fly" through encouragement. It doesn't happen primarily in formal career planning sessions, but on an individual basis due to the open-door policy.

We do have performance evaluations but not a structured look-ahead career planning process. We don't need a formal structure because of our open-door policy and small size. It is an informal, intimate system that just happens.

Pay is tied to profitability, but not by formulaic incentives. It is based on results of the firm's year. What you make is due to judgment. But you always know why you got what you got. We really don't know what anyone else makes, but that's not an issue. We like the fact that there is the flexibility here to get a bigger raise; it's not confined to a set percentage.

Is staff here *required* to have a high level of drive? Not really. It's individually based. You can't prod highly driven people to be more driven. They resent it. On the other hand, enthusiasm and drive are infectious and addictive. You want to be involved with people who make things happen. It comes in waves. It's motivation by being surrounded by enthusiasm and energy, and not by being sat down and told "you need to be energized."

You know you can make an error here, not only on a job but socially as well, and they won't jump on you. Other places are so rigid; you'd never speak freely. Speaking freely allows people to relax and feel comfortable to do their jobs. We laugh at our mistakes and we kid each other. At our annual holiday party we always review our Top Ten Mistakes of the Year.

The way we have been managed has not changed since the beginning and the result is profitability, longevity and low turnover. It fosters continuity both with the clients and personnel. A good summary would be that our success here is due to small size, interest in the individual, empowerment and profitable projects.

Another Middle-Level Group

Here are the comments of a second group at Tramster:

Why is our firm successful? Management instills teamwork. Everyone works together for success of the firm. It's a relaxed atmosphere with management. They interact at all levels. Our leaders have a sense of humor about themselves and about work, and they attract like-minded people.

You know where management is coming from. They don't set

you up. They are good people, the kind you would like to have as neighbors. The impression we have here is that it is not just management out to make a lot of money just for themselves. They want everyone to succeed.

They keep everyone informed. They share the misery. They don't hesitate to jump in and help. Although everyone knows the hierarchy, everyone does everything. They'll do their own photocopying. Everyone will collate and staple if it's got to get done.

Management here is made up of high-integrity people. They won't hurt people. There is no dictatorship; they are very open. They encourage group decisions. Everyone knows why a decision is made.

They are willing to bend. They don't necessarily have to do everything by the book. They treat all employees and clients in a respectful manner. They give the benefit of the doubt.

Derogatory statements don't happen here! In conversations, leaders reflect who they are. Everyone gets lots of exposure to the leaders so they know who they are. They go out and get beat up by the clients the same as we do.

We operate on the principles of trust, respect and integrity. They do what they say they are going to do. They keep their promises. I have previously had bosses that, when you walk out of their office, you want to take a shower. You have a slimy feeling. You just know you are going to be or are being used; maybe stabbed in the back. You can feel the insincerity. Not here.

You have the feeling that the firm needs you. Most people who get hired here are referred by one of the existing employees. A natural selection process has occurred. It's the "genetic tree of our firm."

On the other hand, due to our small size, you can't get out of things. There is no hiding from accountability. Usually, at most other places there are fixed, team-assigned roles, and people act as if the limits of their responsibility end at the boundaries of their role. Accountability goes away. That doesn't happen here. Teams share joint responsibility for getting things done. However, people who don't fit into a particular team can change teams with no bad mark.

There is something about accountability here that is unique; it is shared all the way to the top. No one is afraid of not getting something or of failing as long as they have tried. Around here, you are allowed to learn from your mistakes without retribution. Not trying is the only sin.

This accountability by everyone creates an incentive for people to a point that they feel satisfaction and you just know that everyone is going to do 110 percent. If you don't get awarded a proposal you know that your work wasn't in vain. You know everyone has given their all and that is respected.

There are no hidden agendas here. Political behavior undermines getting work done. If someone who is political gets hired by mistake, they don't last. They can't function in our environment. They leave here naturally. Everyone blends, no matter who does what. Everyone works with different people. Teams assemble and disband as projects come about. People can develop different skills and experience different things.

One of our secrets is lunch. It's a venue where everyone gets a sense of everyone else's life outside of work. People really look forward to lunch together.

You role model yourself. You must be things yourself that you expect others to be. Management gets teamwork by tolerating nothing else. They have willingness to tackle noncompliance. Here, they set a standard and they live that standard. People fire themselves if they don't get it and if they see that they don't fit in. Intolerance is carried out by the culture of our organization. Because of the environment, employees care. We care about the business. We aren't waiting for the official end of the day so we can leave.

We give prompt response to clients. People here check voice mail and e-mails even on nights and weekends and get back to clients promptly. Our culture of being in teams inside creates a natural tendency to deal with clients using interpersonal skills.

Our culture is "Work is not the most important thing in life.

Work is just an important part of the mix." The secrets to this place are character, respect and integrity.

So, what do you think? Did the CEO and the staff say the same things or different things? What do you think is generalizable from this case study? How do you think the comments on these topics would differ in your firm? Would the differences be desirable or undesirable?

I'll summarize the lessons of all of our case studies at the end of the book, but it's worth pausing to reflect on the things that caught my attention when conducting the interviews at this firm. (As hinted above, I suggest you make a note or two on what *you* picked up on. It might not be the same list as mine.)

There were a few interesting "systems" that these people described. The ombudsmen system is an intriguing idea, and the separation of performance review meetings from pay decisions is, I think, brilliant. Having lunch together every day may not be feasible everywhere, but you can see the power of the idea!

Beyond the systems, I was brought up short by the reference to management being "good people." Good people? This is a management tactic? Well, yes, these people (senior and junior) seem to think so. They said the key to their success was all about trust, respect and integrity. How many firm managers are selected primarily on these criteria? (Hint: Not enough.)

Finally, I was struck by how diligently this firm managed how the employees dealt with each other. It's not just about how managers treat employees, it's about how employees treat each other. These managers "police" that (although they wouldn't accept that term) and intervene when necessary.

Little of this is common. Let's wait and see how common it is among our other superstar offices.

CHAPTER THREE

How Successful Offices Did It

We now return to the analysis of our database. I identified the 20 percent of the offices that did best on the financial performance index. I then compared how these offices performed on the individual survey questions, relative to the other, less financially successful, offices.

The most striking finding is that the most financially successful offices did better at *virtually everything* (Appendix 5). In 69 out of 74 questions, their average was significantly higher than the rest of the offices, and in the five remaining questions it was also higher, but not significantly so.

Here are top items where the financially successful offices *most* outperformed the rest. The first group of questions contains seven items:

1. Management listens.
2. Management values input.
3. Management is trusted.
4. Managers are good coaches.
5. Management communication is good.
6. Managers practice what they preach.
7. People treat others with respect.

All seven of these items (one-third of the top twenty things that the most successful offices do better than the rest) have to do with the behavior of individual managers, rather than corporate policies. (We shall see this conclusion again in later analyses.)

These may look like simple accomplishments, because the words are so familiar. But it turns out not to be so simple to get your employees to believe that you listen, communicate well, treat people with respect and value input. It is also not so simple to get your employees to agree that they trust you, or to think you are an effective coach.

There are two challenges here to each of us. First, are we sure we *know how* to accomplish these things? And, second, are we in fact *doing* them effectively? In our case studies, we shall try to outline the "how." Whether or not you do them is up to you. But our preliminary evidence suggests that they *do* influence profits!

The next item is particularly fascinating. Financially successful offices do disproportionately well in having their staff believe that "management practices what it preaches." Note that this says nothing about what it is that management actually preaches: The financial benefit comes from the simple fact of being believable and consistent.

That this should be so is, in retrospect, not so surprising. Imagine the opposite, that people think that management does *not* practice what it preaches. This clearly means that management has lost credibility, and this, I have observed, leads quickly to loss of influence. Why should I believe your latest mission statement, articulation of values or visionary strategy when you have consistently failed to live up to them about all of these in the past?

It is hard to energize people if they are being led by someone who declares that they are committed to something and who then behaves in contrary ways. The conclusion could easily be reached that such a person's word cannot be trusted. And it is hard to make money if this is the prevailing view of the leader. Yet many if not most of our offices did only medium-well on this topic! (And many other firms I know do a lot worse!)

Why do so many businesses fail to meet this test? In part, it is because many managers believe that they are demonstrating leadership and creating motivation and energy by *announcing* a vision, a mission or new strategy, something the firm plans to aim at and be, someday. However, leadership does not lie in the *announcement* of a mission, a vision or a strategy, but in the day-in-day-out *operation* of the business in accordance with what was announced. What is exciting and motivating is seeing evidence that we actually are on the journey to something we can believe in. It is the evidence (the practicing), not the vision (the preaching), that is energizing.

Be careful what you preach: Your people will expect you to live up to it, and if you do not, you will be worse off than when you started!

Let's have a brief look at the next set of items in the top twenty questions where the most financially successful offices most outperformed the others:

8. Be the best, not the biggest.
9. Management gets the best work out of everybody.
10. We have high standards for performance.
11. Quality of the professionals is high.
12. Tolerate nothing less than high levels of client service.
13. People do whatever it takes.

This group of questions is clearly about having high standards, which, we shall see, is a prerequisite for making superior profits. Again, notice the challenge. It is not enough that management preach its commitment to high standards, but that they convince the staff that, in the real world of daily operations, this is, in fact, how the office runs. In other words, management does not compromise the standards for expediency purposes. Most people preach high standards. Few resist the temptations of expediency!

These are not statements about achieving competence. Notice the language: Management gets the best work out of *everybody*. We *tolerate nothing less* than high client service. People do *whatever it takes*.

As one tries to absorb the significance of this, remember that the majority of the offices in our study did only modestly well on these scores, and some poorly. Are these shoddy places? Not at all. They wouldn't be in business if they were. They're all solid, competent, "we're as good as anybody else" places.

And that's the point! There is a powerful and meaningful gap between competence and excellence, and the most successful offices exploit that gap. They set *and enforce* high standards, and their employees can see it. This produces profit in two ways: First, there is a direct market and financial benefit when you achieve high quality. Second, the motivating and energizing effect of working in such an environment leads each person to achieve more.

The next two items in our top questions are clear: Successful offices convince their people that they care about the long term:

14. We discuss strategic objectives, not just the financial goals.
15. We invest in the future.

These are simple statements, and one is tempted to move on. But note that these are not trivial accomplishments. If you ask most employees (including partners, where that term is appropriate) whether the business is being run with the future in mind, or whether it is being run on a short-term, quarter-to-quarter basis, you will get the second answer more often than you get the first. The impact on performance should be clear. If the firm is seen by me to be building towards the future, I might be tempted to commit myself, pitch in and do my part. If I think the firm is only worried about the short term, I'm going to worry about my career and not the firm.

So, let's emphasize the key lesson. *The data* (not theory) say that if your employees believe that you are investing for the future and discuss strategic goals, you'll be more likely to be financially successful!

According to our data, financially successful operations also ensure that their people feel that the pay scheme is fair:

16. The compensation system is fair.
17. Those who contribute the most are rewarded.

It is worthwhile noting that these are two separate issues, involving process and content. The issue of perceived compensation fairness has as much to do with the performance evaluation and compensation setting process as it does with the actual dollar decisions. As we shall see in our case studies (and summarize later), what our superstar offices seem to do incredibly well is to run a compensation-setting process that everyone understands and perceives as fair.

So what do these categories of skilled managers, high standards, long-term thinking and fair pay lead to? Here are the last three of the top twenty items that financially superior offices do better than the rest:

18. Enthusiasm and morale are high.
19. People are commited and loyal.
20. People are dedicated.

The most successful offices have measurably more enthusiastic, committed and dedicated people. And if you can't make money from that, you don't deserve to be in business!

It is worth noting (and stressing) that, in absolute terms, "enthusiasm and morale" was the *lowest ranked* among all the questions. We can now answer one part of our earlier question: do employee attitudes matter? Well, we don't yet have *"proof,"* but it is more than a little suggestive that "enthusiasm and morale" (least well done overall) was the single topic on which the financially successful offices most outperformed the rest! Hmmm!

Let's acknowledge that we have not yet *proven* causality. We know that employee attitudes and profits are correlated, but we haven't yet shown which direction the prevailing influence flows. Do profits cause attitudes, or do attitudes cause profits?

The answer is given in chapter 9, but let's discuss it a little here.

That profits raise enthusiasm cannot be denied. But look at some of the other relationships we have found. We've seen that there is a relationship between profits and having high standards of performance. In which way do you think that influence flows?

Do more profitable firms then set higher standards of performance, or do they first set high standards and then get the profits? Do firms first get profitable, and then manage so that they get the best work out of everybody, or do they manage people and then get the profits? We can't be definitive yet, but my guess should be clear to you: Profits are more of a consequence than they are a cause. But form your own tentative hypothesis, and let's continue our explorations.

Table 3–1: Factor Scores of Most Successful Offices

Factor (Question Group)	Scores of Top 20 Percent as a Percent of the Rest
Commitment, enthusiasm, and respect	+10.6
Fair compensation	+9.4
Long-term orientation	+7.2
Quality and client relationships	+6.3
Employee satisfaction	+6.1
Coaching	+5.4
High standards	+5.0
Training and development	+4.3
Empowerment	+3.7

Here's one more way to summarize what we've seen. Table 3–1 lists the scores (on the 1-to-6 disagree/agree scale) of offices in the top 20 percent (financially) on each of our nine factors or question groups, compared to the rest. All of these differences are statistically significant, except for the difference in the training and development scores. It is readily apparent what the best are achieving that the others are not: The top three are commitment, enthusiasm, and respect; fair compensation; and long-term orientation.

To make sure we are clear, here are the individual questions contained in the top three groups in this table (the others being given in Appendix 3.)

Commitment, Enthusiasm and Respect

❑ Enthusiasm and morale around here have never been higher.
❑ Management of our office is successful in fostering commitment and loyalty.
❑ This is a fun place to work.
❑ People within our office always treat others with respect.
❑ We have no room for those who put their individual interests ahead of the interests of the clients or the office.
❑ Management gets the best work out of everybody in the office.

Fair Compensation

❑ Considering my contribution, I think I am paid fairly compared to others in the office.
❑ Those who contribute the most to the overall success of the office are the most highly rewarded.
❑ Considering the office as a whole, the compensation system is managed equitably and fairly.

Long-Term Orientation

❑ I know exactly what my office is trying to achieve strategically.
❑ We maintain a balance between short- and long-term goals.
❑ We regularly discuss our progress toward our strategic objectives, not just the financial goals.
❑ We invest a significant amount of time in things that will pay off in the future.
❑ The emphasis in our office is on long-term success, rather than short-term results.

Notice that the premium achieved on these things by the successful offices is not, on average, that large. What might be considered modest improvements (5 to 10 percent) in office averages seem to be enough to be associated with dramatically better financial results. There is hope!

CHAPTER FOUR

Northport: A Case Study

Northport is an international public relations firm. In this chapter we will listen to the people of their New York office, which achieved a financial performance 52 percent above the average for all the offices in our database. They doubled their profit in two years, and achieved a profit per employee some 80 percent above the norm. Here, in descending order, are the ten areas in which they most outperformed the average on the employee survey, by amounts ranging from 18 to 50 percent.

1. We have high-quality training opportunities to improve skills.
2. Management shows by their actions that employee training is important.
3. Around here you are required, not just encouraged, to learn and develop new skills.
4. Enthusiasm and morale around here have never been higher.
5. We have an effective system in place to measure client feedback.
6. This place has done a good job of providing the training I've needed to do my job well.
7. I am actively helped with my personal development.
8. I am given the chance at the office to learn and develop new skills.

9. We keep our people informed about what is happening in the office.
10. We regularly discuss our progress toward our strategic objectives, not just the financial goals.

As before, we listen both to top management and mid-level professionals. We first listen to their executive committee talk:

What are we doing to get our results? Most of our time as an executive committee is spent on HR issues. As a firm, we have been measuring employee attitudes and concerns via a survey since 1991, very early in the firm's life. The staff takes the surveys very seriously, and they know we do too. We make complete disclosure of the results, and give a formal two-hour presentation to all employees.

We put out a written highlight report as well. We then have individual group meetings to zero in on issues of importance to each specific group. We make public commitments about the initiatives and actions. The staff knows the surveys are important because they affect what goes on. For example, one survey showed our salaries weren't up to market levels and people wanted us to address salaries. And we did.

Morale here *is* very high. We hire fabulous people, and we explicitly hire for enthusiasm, excitement, and sparks. We are also selective about clients. We try to keep only those that are exciting. We will walk away from clients if we question whether we can work with them—if it is not fun, creative or exciting. Employees give us big points for this. It is easier nowadays to replace clients than good employees.

We work long, hard hours, so we are inevitably a big part of the staff's social life. Social connections lead to a more team-based atmosphere. People nowadays are looking for a community where they work. It is more than having Fun Fridays. We offer French lessons, outings, a book-readers club and many other events. The interactions among employees that result from these make for meaningful work relationships.

We have a monthly all-staff meeting, designed to be a business update and to allow the teams a chance to look at what went right or wrong in a nonthreatening atmosphere. We take the opportunity to have a giggle. Each month one of our groups is responsible for running the meeting. There is usually a theme, with decorations, and prizes. This all builds a team spirit, which makes money for us, we have no doubt.

If someone is not a team player here, even if they are good technically, they don't survive. Everyone here is expected to be self-motivated and vibrant. If we make a mistake and hire an individual who isn't these things, the team starts to exclude that person long before the manager picks up on it. It's a self-correcting process that takes place naturally. A client once said they liked our firm because they knew that "No one has a private agenda" and they could speak to anyone on team and would be helped. That's worth a lot of money.

We have a more rigorous career development approach than other firms. Orientation is thorough. We have a six-week "how is it going meeting?" then three months, then six months. These are done very formally in this office compared to other offices of our firm.

We are also rigorous about on-time performance reviews. If they don't get done on time, a person's raise doesn't go through. If a manager neglects to do the career development review stuff, his or her own bonus is reduced significantly.

Coaching programs are held regularly. People need feedback all the time, as well as in-depth guidance of how to develop. As we get bigger, we have used some programs from outside the firm to help us develop coaching skills in our senior managers. This is very expensive but we're sure it's worth it.

If a manager were not a good coach, financial consequences would occur. In the long run, lack of coaching skill would not be tolerated. But we go to great lengths to save such a person, such as hiring a personal coach to help them.

We regularly ask employees whether they have good role models in the office, and we have been getting higher scores every year. We think this is a central element of our success.

We must give our managers and other senior people the skills needed to retain the best employees, especially in this people crisis we are experiencing. We have large clients looking for longer-term relationships and it is essential that we maintain teams to keep the clients happy and satisfied. Savvy clients appreciate a team that grows with them.

Each manager's job is to balance client service, employee development and business health. Even though it's difficult, this is not rocket science. We are doing good, obvious management stuff. What is different here is that we are actually enforcing it and there are consequences if managers don't do it. This is not a loose environment despite the fun things we try to do.

We are organized and have good financial controls in place. There is a lot of structure. After employees get through the first few months they appreciate the structure, because the systems that are in place are designed to run the business in an efficient, profitable and fun way. This means a more disciplined office. The trick is to find the right combination of fun and discipline that gets the job done.

We practice financial transparency with the staff. Except for salaries, we discuss everything financial with managers on a quarterly basis, and this material gets passed down to employees. We let everyone know the hard numbers. This also shows our commitment to making money as well as having fun. We have other points of transparency via job descriptions, salary ranges, and so on. A phrase commonly used around here is: Treat People Like Grown-Ups. We know from working with recruiters that in other places information is controlled. Here it is transparent.

With regard to training, we live the promise. We manage it and worry about it. We really do listen to input from employees and adjust programs to make sure we are getting the training we want. A minimum of thirty hours per person per year is required, and a training stipend is given to each person. Those who don't use it are spoken to. Our approach to training has evolved, but it is at the core of our culture. We don't cancel training if profits are down.

There is an approval process to make sure the training we do is appropriate, but we interpret that liberally. For example, we have even approved acting lessons to help someone improve presentation skills and provided voice training for the same purpose.

We want people to manage their work and clients around their training. We must be able to say to a client, "So-and-so can't come to your meeting because she has training scheduled." Most clients accept (and even approve of) this.

We are big on self-responsibility. We once had a problem with people not showing up to an outside training course for which the firm had prepaid. We asked the employees what to do about this. They decided that if an employee didn't show up, part of their stipend would go to pay for it.

This isn't meant to be punitive, but self-correcting, and is part of the grown-up environment we strive for. It means a sense of responsibility to the firm and to themselves to grow their role here. There is no spoonfeeding. We expect people to step up to the plate, and fix their problems without waiting for someone to tell them to do it. We hire people who know how to take responsibility. People feel they are in control of where they are going clientwise and careerwise.

We try to minimize politics. We discourage gossip, whining, complaining. There is not a lot of idle chatter here. There's a lot of "Why?" We will stop the engines to fix things. When we can't fix something, we are open with people about this as well. We are diligent in keeping promises, because it is a violation of trust if we don't.

Staff development is a huge part of our client service, since the client is getting highly skilled people. A client once said "We don't want your A team, they will excel before we do. Can we have the B or C team instead?" We didn't get that job (and frankly we didn't want it) because we build our pitches around a "we are the best" attitude and if the client doesn't want that or can't work that way, then it is best we don't work with the client.

We have an annual client survey and we consistently have at least one face-to-face with each client every year. For an individual client, we have the team fill out the same form. We have a feedback session with the staff afterwards. The managers take the results back to the team to report what is being done well, what done badly. The document then goes back to the client and we make a commitment to the client, identifying problems and developing an action plan to fix things. The whole team is involved in how to fix things.

Survey results are combined and given to the management team to show overall what the positives and negatives are. We publish aggregate client feedback results internally, and bonuses are influenced by client feedback results. We have regular reviews where each team has to write up three things that keep them awake at night about their client.

Then we have "The Doctor Is In" sessions. Any team can bring in a technical or client problem they are having. For each problem the "doctors" (three senior managers who have had special sensitivity training as facilitators) then spend 15 minutes doing fast brainstorming of ideas.

Our management acts as a team. Things are brainstormed, decisions are made collectively and everything is put out on the table. This style transfers to the employees. There are no politics here. Everyone cares as much about everyone else's group. We see goals as collective; no egos allowed. Politicking wouldn't be tolerated.

We have no room for people who want to cruise because both peers and managers would be troubled by it. Sometimes you have to actually tell someone, "You have to contribute some ideas around here to move ahead." Usually, people realize they are not pulling their weight, and they say "OK" and change. On the other hand, we have different ways of rewarding people, like spot bonuses.

In the past, people who left the firm were treated as pariahs. Bad treatment of those leaving had a hugely negative impact on those who stayed. It was like a double standard. If you were leaving, all of a sudden you were treated as less than a human. People realized that if they were to leave too they would get that treatment from "their firm" as well.

That part of our culture has changed. Now we treat people who leave respectfully and with appreciation for what they have done for our firm. We have goodbye parties, sending people away respectfully, with their contributions highlighted. The result is that we have former employees who actually want to come back.

There are no surprises here for the employee. We are articulate in saying, "This is what we stand for and this is what you get." We practice what we preach. We stick to our guns, and there is no wishy-washy management behavior. We are disciplined about standards, although we are open to reasons why they may not be met.

It takes emotional courage to be a good and improving manager. Even if it is intellectually obvious what has to be done, it is still hard to do it. It is about respect, trust, empowerment, confidence, loyalty, keeping promises. It's about having a certain type of character, having principles and sticking to them. We have learned that sticking to your principles has a tight correlation with profitability. Ethics have to be the bedrock that you start from.

The Middle-Level Group

Now we hear from Northport's middle-level group. Those who volunteered to talk were representative of a variety of departments and were all at a junior level with exception of one newly hired VP. Here's what they had to say:

What is being done here that causes positive results? People are willing and eager to stay at work, due both to a great corporate culture and to a sense of community.

Around here, you are required to respect your colleagues and be cordial. If you are "snappish" with someone, you *have* to apologize to him or her, whether he or she is a more senior or a lower level person. If people don't treat others with respect, they are discharged, no matter how senior or successful.

It's different in other firms. Some even allow people to scream at the staff, using obscene language, which we would never accept! Management has also resigned clients who do not show respectful treatment to us.

Our rule is "Give respect and you will get it." You hear "Thank you's" every day. Management knows that in today's environment any of us can go somewhere else at any time (and probably for more money). They show appreciation, not just with money but in small ways like sharing between teams and e-mail "thank you's."

Management lets us be the best judge of our own priorities. We respect everyone's ideas and values. We listen to everyone. We don't give people the brush-off because they are at a different level. Everyone brings expertise to the table, and you must be able to identify and use that expertise.

We are a tight community here. We play hard and work hard. It provides a fun environment to a stressful occupation. You must take the time to interact socially, even if just in the hallway.

There is more freedom here than other places. There is flexibility here about what you want, what you want to work on and what your personal issues are. Whatever you are doing or what is going on, you'll be listened to!

We have a willingness to let someone young take on a job and be responsible. Age doesn't matter. Management asks for feedback from all levels of people on a regular basis, whether it's a dinner menu or a client program. They create task forces for all changes in the firm.

For example, when we moved office space, everyone's opinion was sought out. Everyone feels free to say, "This is not going to work," no matter what level you are at. Most importantly, we can see how feedback changes things here. You know management is listening.

We have constant innovation and change. There is no "This is how it's been done here!" There's always a chance to break new ground. We push to be on the leading edge, always trying to do something else, always building on what works. There's always a risk here and that is motivating. It would be hard for a cruiser to fit in here because the review process is always about "Where do you want to go next? What are the resources that you need?"

Management is trusted because they are available. Managers support and back up their staff and the staff's decisions. They are willing to confront the client on our behalf. They understand that employees are looking for help from managers in growing their career.

Personal life is respected. If you work late, they understand that you will be in late the next day. Teams that are overbooked are told not to pursue new business. Clear workload and revenue targets exist but there are no brownie points for exceeding them. Our top manager once told us, "Profitability is too high, and it shows we are working too hard." That had a big impact!

There is clearly a commitment to the development of staff. Management understands you may not be here forever but they want to make sure you have skills. We think this is very noble.

The head of the office is real and honorable. She is not soft; she just doesn't put walls between people. What you see is what you get. You see the real person all of the time. She is, however, also a "let's get down to business" person and can be hardnosed.

It's the little things. On your anniversary of your time with the firm, you get a note from her—handwritten. People actually post her notes on their walls. She knows everyone's name. When you first come in you have tea with her and talk about yourself. She is personally involved with the staff.

What do we do differently on the client side? Reasonable deadlines are given to clients. This is very much appreciated by the staff, and it makes for a better quality of work.

We tell clients we have a whole team and everyone is important and can answer their questions. This is good for the clients, because they know who is doing their work and that their questions will be addressed promptly. We also believe that whoever pitches the work also does the work. That is not necessarily the case in other places.

Recently, one of us didn't want to work on a specific account which concerned gun advocacy. He would have to do work for something he didn't believe in, and it upset him. Management agreed they didn't believe in the message and therefore couldn't service the account properly, so they resigned the account. We believe you must believe in what you are doing.

Creativity here is second to none. If someone from another department has an idea, they are welcome to join our brainstorm sessions. We make a lot of use of cross-boundary teams.

We use the right staff levels for accounts and billing. Our upper rate isn't charged if someone from lower level can do work. We play fair with the clients, and they know it. They can see it.

Pitches [new business proposals] are sold on the basis of relationships. You want to like the people you are pitching the program to, and you want them to like you, not just the work. Winning business is about relationships, about who the client will trust.

This is a nice environment to work in and that is why many nice people are here. This image transcends to clients with whom some relationships have been as long as twenty-seven years. Our people have gone on site and actually worked temporarily for the client company, while still in our employ. We think it shows the client's respect for us.

Face-to-face client reviews are done annually. This allows open integrity and respect. The results of client feedback help you know how you are doing and help you to do your job.

Bonuses are tied to what you are doing, and are more frequent rather than annual. They are tied to something concrete and specific, so you can understand why you got it.

What is one thing we could improve on? Salaries should be brought up to industry standards. Everyone knows that if you leave you can get 15 to 20 percent more somewhere else. We are happy to be here but happiness doesn't pay the bills. However, management isn't ignoring this problem, so that helps to make people want to stay.

We are two hundred people here now and we don't want the firm to get any bigger. They do a lot to keep you in the loop here and they don't want to lose the family-like atmosphere, which can happen when you get bigger.

As always with these profiles of superstar offices, I invite you to reflect on what you think the lessons are. Here are my initial reactions:

I walked away from these interviews with one word ringing in my brain: "Wow!" Here's a group of people who know exactly what they're doing and how to do it. Did you notice that terrific phrase? "The right combination of fun and discipline." That's one to remember.

The fun stuff is real and pervasive here: book clubs, have a giggle, theme-decorated meetings. And, notice, it's not just fun periodically at the annual retreat or office meeting. It's fun embedded in how they conduct their business. But let's also not ignore the discipline. Managers don't get their bonuses if they don't do performance reviews? That's tough! (And courageous and brilliant!)

Most firms today have client feedback of one sort or another, but how many take as disciplined an approach as this office? Full debriefings, share the result with all of the team, and make public commitments to the client about how you are going to follow up! Now, that's discipline! That's courage! That's practicing what you preach!

And by the way, we did hear those topics again, as we did in chapter 2: The employees think their manager is noble and honorable! How crucial is that? (Very!) How common is it? (Not very!)

Finally, note that the concern about not getting too big exists at this 200-person operation, as well as in the smaller operations in our other case studies. Everyone thinks you have to be small to sustain a culture, but maybe it's not a requirement. Two hundred people is pretty big, at least for the businesses explored here.

CHAPTER FIVE

Correlations with Financial Performance

In chapter 3, we compared the best with the rest, the most financially successful offices with the rest of the database. The limitation of this approach is that it doesn't tell us much about what happens if you are not yet a superstar, but do make improvements from, say, weak to average on important things. Does that have an impact, or do you have to reach superstar levels for the benefit to be seen?

It would really help us to know, for example, whether improving on an item like "We have an uncompromising determination to achieve excellence in all that we do" is associated with improved financial performance across the *entire* range of performance, high to low.

The answer is that yes, striving for excellence is associated with improvement across the entire range! So much so, in fact, that (as we shall see in this chapter) fully 23 percent of all the variations in financial performance (across geography, lines of business, size of firm) can be explained by the employees' answers to this one question. That's high!

Think of it this way. If the only thing you knew about an office was the response to this one question, knowing nothing about what business it was in, its size or its country of operation, you'd still be about one-quarter, or 23 percent, of the way to being able to understand its financial results. That's quite a long way!

Questions of this type are addressed by using a standard statistical calculation, the correlation coefficient, which measures the ex-

tent to which two variables tend to move up and down together—
that is, a change in one (a survey question) is usually associated with
a change in the other (financial performance).

Nearly all of the survey questions show a measurable relationship to financial performance. To be precise, 85 percent of the questions displayed a statistically significant (positive) correlation with
the financial performance of the office. (For detailed statistics, see
Appendix 6.)

The twenty questions most highly correlated with financial performance are shown here. The first eight strike a similar theme, one
that we saw in our first, more simple analysis in chapter 3. All are
about the achievement (and enforcement) of high standards:

1. *We have an uncompromising determination to achieve excellence in everything we do.*
2. *We have a real commitment to high-quality work, and
   tolerate nothing less.*
3. *We have a real commitment to high levels of client service, and tolerate nothing else.*
4. *The quality of service delivered to clients by my group is
   consistently high.*
5. *The quality of work performed for clients by my group is
   consistently high.*
6. *In this office we set and enforce very high standards for
   performance.*
7. *Management gets the best work out of everybody in the
   office.*
8. *The quality of the professionals in our office is as high as
   can be expected.*

Every firm preaches this stuff, but that's not the finding. The data
speak: If your employees agree that you *actually practice* these policies, you'll make more money! True excellence wins!

The second group of questions that are highly correlated with financial performance all have to do with client relationships:

9. *We keep clients informed on issues affecting their business.*
10. *We make our clients feel as if they're important to us.*
11. *Client satisfaction is a top priority at our firm.*
12. *We listen well to what the client has to say.*

Notice how much of this relates to quality and client relationships. Remember, our findings are *not* that people management alone is exclusively important. As we said in the Introduction, conventional wisdom is right in saying that great client service gets results. (We've just seen some proof.) However, we are also seeing (and will see more) that quality and great client service are themselves products of other things (a fact that we will demonstrate even more thoroughly in chapter 9).

Let's continue down the list of things highly correlated with financial performance, across the full range of performance.

Next, we again see the importance of pay schemes:

13. *Those who contribute the most to the overall success of the office are the most highly rewarded.*

Notice that this doesn't suggest what the pay scheme should be. The determining factor is just whether the people think it rewards the right people. (This is another example of practicing what you preach. It says the dollars are, in fact, flowing in accordance with the commonly understood performance criteria. There are no surprises and no disconnects.)

Next comes another item we have already seen: the importance of a long-term orientation:

14. *We maintain a balance between short- and long-term goals.*
15. *The emphasis in our office is on long-term success, rather than short-term results.*
16. *We invest a significant amount of time in things that will pay off in the future.*

17. *The actions of our firm are consistent with our strategic objectives and mission statement.*

Finally, we see high correlations for the following statements:

18. *Our team is effective at achieving our desired results.*
19. *I am committed to this firm as a career opportunity.*
20. *There are real opportunities here for meaningful career and professional advancement.*

The themes are pretty clear, aren't they? Enforcing high standards, including quality and uncompromising client service appear to have the strongest relationship with the overall financial proficiency of the office. Nothing's so profitable as quality work and service.

But it's not quite as simple as that. We're not done yet. What we now need to ask is, what are the successful offices (and their management) actually doing that *produces* such high-quality work and service? We already have some clues, and we will find out more in subsequent chapters.

Analysis of Factors

It is important to stress the fact (already noted) that 85 percent of the questions (i.e., almost *everything* in our survey) are measurably correlated to the long-term financial success of the office. To try to achieve clarity, let's look at our nine factors.

Our nine factors, computed by grouping similar questions together, prove definitely that no one cultural aspect of an office is uniquely responsible for the financial performance of that office.

As Table 5–1 shows, *all* the factors have a statistically significant relationship with financial performance. Six of the nine factors can each explain more than 10 percent of the overall variation in financial performance.

Table 5–1: Correlations of Factors with Financial Performance

Factor	Percent of Variation in Financial Performance Explained by Each Factor
Quality and client relationships	24 percent
Fair compensation	15 percent
Long-term orientation	15 percent
Employee satisfaction	13 percent
Coaching	12 percent
Commitment, enthusiasm and respect	11 percent
High standards	9 percent
Training and development	6 percent
Empowerment	4 percent

What we are seeing here is that while some factors (such as quality and client relationships) have a major relationship to financial performance, others also have a measurable influence. Focusing on the client marketplace alone (as important as that is) is not a sufficient recipe for success. There are other ingredients necessary to make the cake rise.

Given the evidence we have looked at so far, we have glimpses of what the essential, individual ingredients may be. Later chapters will look at all the ingredients together, so that we can judge what the set of ingredients and the proportions really need to be.

CHAPTER SIX

Mustang Communications: A Case Study

Here's another of our superstar offices that achieved both astoundingly high financial performance and superior employee attitude scores. Mustang, a 220-person office in a multioffice firm, obtained a financial performance 47 percent above the norm, driven by outstanding margins and a rapid growth in profit. Here are the ten items on the employee survey, in descending order, where it most outperformed other offices (by 20 to 61 percent.)

1. We have high-quality training opportunities to improve skills.
2. Management shows by their actions that employee training is important.
3. This place has done a good job of providing the training I've needed to do my job well.
4. I am actively helped with my personal development.
5. Around here you are required, not just encouraged, to learn and develop new skills.
6. Enthusiasm and morale around here has never been higher.
7. Management of our office is successful in fostering commitment and loyalty.
8. We make unusual efforts to identify and recruit the best people for every job.

9. We keep our people informed about what is happening in the office.
10. There are real opportunities here for meaningful career and professional advancement.

Here's the office leadership explaining what they do:

The key to our success is that we have teams that have worked together for a long time, in a business where longevity is not common. Longevity builds credibility. It allows you to build true trust. There is a willingness to take more risks (upward or downward) because you know the other person will be there to deal with again and again.

As management, we do our job with passion, but also with a compassionate style. This means making decisions with your heart *and* your head. We try to make decisions that are in the best interest of the whole firm community.

Before I took over as office head I took a six-week sabbatical, which is a firmwide benefit. This turned out to coincide with the time period when my two lieutenants were both taking maternity leave. They went off, yet I was still permitted to take my sabbatical while they were on leave. And I was made head of the office when I returned! This not only built my loyalty, but a lot of other people noticed how supportive the firm was.

But it's not just about being supportive. We have a meritocracy here. We take performance seriously. People get tired of other people who don't hold up their end of the deal. You either get the work done or you don't. You own it or not. All of us know who can do the work and we know it will get done.

Our people are long-term oriented because we have a recognized culture of being reliable. If you take something on, then you deliver. We also stress the importance of learning from your mentor, at all levels.

We are apolitical here. If anyone becomes political, they are gone. We once hired a senior person from a major competitor, which is known for its politics. She seemed to think that success is based on serving the client at the cost of everyone else. She brutalized her staff, and we quickly caught on to her horrible behavior. We checked with her clients, who said they liked her.

But we fired her anyway, because our philosophy is that we do great work and treat people well. It's not one or the other. It took us one and a half years to sort it out, but we got there. It was worth enduring the difficulties during this period so that people could see that while we deal with problems, we give everyone a fair chance.

We have a great depth of talent here. We hire ahead of demand if necessary. Depth of talent lets you service bigger and more de-manding clients. It makes it easier to recruit. I am not always forced to use the same people. Since I have options, this gives me more freedom, as a manager, to avoid short-term thinking.

It makes money because of the quality of client you attract, the potential for growth, and the flexibility to do new things. I often think of managing as like an act on the Ed Sullivan show. How many plates can you keep spinning at once?

We believe that you build your people and the rest will come. You can't just manage for the numbers. You put people in a place where they are excited, pay them well and train them well. The wealth will follow.

I regularly ask our employees who is the one person who is the magnet for them to stay. Hopefully, most will name a top manage-ment person. The key to attracting good people and retaining them is having magnet people in place. Also, you must ask, "Is there anyone here who would make you want to leave?" Senior managers should be the reason people want to stay, and all too often they are not.

You must be hands-off and let people do their work, as long as they realize there is structure in the place. We have a system of staff sharing. We distribute a sheet each month indicating the percent-ages of time everyone is expected to bill. If someone is low, we arrange for him or her to go to another group for a while. The sys-tem doesn't need a lot of my input, because all the department managers below me take joint responsibility for the whole office.

We also work hard at developing our people. One of our managers created a two-day course (with a colleague from another office). It attempts to teach us new, practical ways to do our work and gives us real tools, methodologies and forms to run our accounts. We realized that we had just assumed that certain things were being done when in actuality they were not. So, the result was usable guidelines. It's been a big success. I didn't have to initiate that. It bubbled up.

Our training courses are run like a college, all voluntary. People make their own choices and courses can get filled up. We hold a pep rally at the beginning of the school year. It sounds hokey, but people realize that the firm is serious about it and that it is something we have made a financial investment in.

Training works best when insiders do it and they are committed to what they do. It is an embarrassment if your course doesn't work out well. I prefer one-third outside instructors and two-thirds inside people doing the training. Outside people bring external stimulation, but inside people allow role modeling, leadership, and group visibility to filter down.

We hold regular staff meetings. Once a month, all of our 220 people go to a local club for a meeting. We celebrate anniversaries at the firm. We promote people by having their supervisor giving a two-minute personal testimony about the person, in any way they wish (a video tribute, flowers, or song, whatever they want to do). The texture and emotion of these presentations are incredible. These meetings are an opportunity for us to showcase our best work for everyone to see. We announce new hires and read their bios. We take questions.

We have new-hire lunches. We also hold informal lunchtime chats with a random group of about 22 people from all levels, an idea originally suggested through an employee survey. We have monthly group meetings and practice meetings (of our four groups), held to address business issues.

We try to show visible leadership. That mostly means being readily accessible and available to employees to help solve client and business problems, but it also means that we walk the floors and say "Thank you." Managers need to acknowledge, recognize and appreciate what is going on, regularly and continuously.

We have a TGIM Group (Thank God It's Monday). This is a group of staff people with a human resources advisor. It is dedicated to making this a better and more enjoyable place to work. They have a budget to work with, and it is taken very seriously. Some of the things they have arranged include onsite massages, manicures, shoeshines, happy hours, weight watcher meetings, Tai Bo, exercise classes, ice cream sundaes, gifts on Mothers Day, even Valentine's Day. They do something on all Hallmark holidays (but not religious ones). They conducted a Spring Break where they transformed the restaurant across the street into a beach party atmosphere. This was a party to reward everyone after a particularly hard stretch of work.

The result of all this is motivation and retention. There have been cynics regarding all this, but we have seen those cynics turn into believers over time. Merchandising ourselves to the staff works and is important to the overall success of the office. I like to think of it as creating "Moments of Fun." Work is not always fun. Clients don't always say thank you. Therefore, a high point in the day is when someone shows levity and a good sense of humor.

We are trusted (as management) because we like our people. We are nice to them. They can trust us to look out for them, often at the sacrifice of ourselves. Our ambitions don't overtake everyone else's. Our agenda is making this a great place to work rather than our own star rising. We make decisions in the best interest of our people.

As an illustration, we had a plan to give one of our rising stars a spot bonus. Before we could get the check cut something very negative happened on his account. But, we still gave him the bonus (to his big surprise) to show appreciation of his hard work, to show loyalty to him, and show our confidence in his work.

Of course, being nice isn't enough. Today, employees say, "Okay, you gave me ice cream. That's nice. But where are my stock options?" It takes high recognition, plus psychic rewards plus monetary rewards. We have psychic rewards and monetary rewards now that in the olden days never existed.

We have tried to create a firm where people will want to build a career. We are not in it for the short term. Decisions are aimed at the long term. Other places only care about short-term growth and profits. If you are a manager who doesn't plan to stay long, then you don't care (on a short-term basis) how you hire. But, if you think you are going to stay somewhere for a long time, you make much more thoughtful decisions. We think this is the difference between Mustang and other places.

If a client abuses our people, we gracefully resign the account. Based on this thinking, we have turned down significant opportunities. Also, if we know we are going to fail with a client, we don't accept the job. We look for continuous growth with a client and not a short-term job.

How do we recognize when hiring how to get people with the right mentality? It is difficult. Most of the time it is a gut check. I ask questions like "What kind of people do you like to work for? What kind of people do you like working for you?" I check for eye contact. I say to myself, "Is this someone I could consider a friend?" You have to find a shared value system with the person.

We interview by teams. Often a junior assistant account manager will interview a potential senior VP. By the time anyone gets here it is a win-win.

We have a lot of boomerangs, people who leave us and then rejoin us a short while later. This is a place you know you can return to. People get out and their experience with other firms is such that they realize that we have a world-class, first-class place to work.

What is our number one most important management tool? We know how to throw a good party! This can retain people and increase billability by 15 percent! Yes, we're serious!

You've got to work hard with your people and play hard. People like and need a release. They like to see management loosen up. We like people who like to dance, literally. These are people we can work with.

The summary I'd give is that our firm has the ability to think and bet on the long term. Part of strategy is not only having that good business idea but also having the guts to stick with it.

Middle-Level Group

Now we listen to a group of mid-level professionals at Mustang. Here is their view of the place:

This place focuses on its people. Our management regularly interviews all levels. They care about where the people have come from and where they are going.

As a mid-level team leader you get judged on creating a collaborative culture for your team, not only by doing the work but also by being a sounding board for your team.

Our mentality is to be people who are open-minded and can roll with the punches. People who just want a job fail here. If you stay here, you are constantly asked, "Are you happy with what you are doing? Do you want to work on other pieces of business?" You have to be enthusiastic. You have to want to grow.

Management works hard to find out what people like and they try to be accommodating. Employees can say what they want to do next. Management listens, and while it is a gradual process, they try to accommodate you and they explain what's happening along the way.

We save (a lot) on recruitment and retention costs. If people are happy and have a chance to do what they want to do, they will be superworkers. They work more enthusiastically and are more productive. And they're more likely to stay.

We also benefit from long-standing relationships with clients when we have lower turnover. The sequence is: Good people management leads to longevity which leads to trust relationships with clients, which leads to more business.

We always put focus on the other person. We ask each other and clients: What do you want? People who stay here have a personal interest in this place and care about what they do.

Management leads by example. They do provide incentives and they give good raises. But they also pay attention. They give pats on the back, spot bonuses. Our top manager is always walking the hall. Her enthusiasm is contagious. She will bend over backwards to make this a good place. You know you are appreciated. All the managers practice this. You are proud to be here.

Clients say "I like working with you people. You know my business as well as anyone, even more than some of our own people." Caring about the client is part of our work ethic. At lots of places, the feeling is that the client is the enemy. Here, if there is an adversarial relationship with the client, the firm gets rid of the client. It is great to have that commitment behind you. Here we try to help our clients solve their most pressing issues. At other places it is *sell, sell, sell!*

We have chosen to have a smaller client roster, but with roots deeper in each relationship. We are the dandelions of our industry. You can then have more credibility with the clients. They buy into your strategy. They have confidence in you. If you hire more people for their account they believe that you are doing the right thing by them. Clients reward good work by giving more assignments to the firm.

Our managers are amazingly brilliant people. They are smart, but human. They don't talk down to you. There is an open-door policy. They make time for you. They listen and they allow themselves to have open minds.

It is an intense experience to work here. You get wrapped up in what you are doing and you don't want to break away. You can't break away.

As everyone knows, this is a difficult era for recruiting people. But even in this climate we won't sacrifice and hire just anybody. We hire to fit the culture. We'll say "no" if a person won't blend. We would rather wait and get the right person.

An office takes on the personality of the people leading it. Here it is collaboration first. This squishy stuff is not a trade-off with hard work. It keeps you working hard and it keeps you committed to the firm and to the client. Just to be here, many people join us at a lower level than their previous position. They take a step back to go forward. They can see the promise here.

At staff meetings they do talk about numbers. They give us the plan. They communicate and empower. They keep you informed. The message is "We are all in this together." Everybody hears it. You know where the office stands in performance and you know where you fit. This makes junior-level staff better business people. People need to know how the business runs.

We have a sabbatical leave program, when you can do whatever you want. It is the gift of time. After you complete seven years, you get two months fully paid. This benefit is available to anyone in any position who works in this firm.

Management is willing to take money from the profits to fund employee happiness. This says to the staff: "We will risk part of our profits and it will be made up by results it gets from rising profits and repeat business." This saves on turnover. It is a good investment.

We have in-house training, our own college and tuition reimbursement for outside courses. You are encouraged to do training but it is not required. They do monitor the training and people can take courses in anything they want as long as it is somehow related to the business.

We have a 360-degree review system. Communication is crucial, both ways. It is a two-way street here.

This is a fun place. A committee arranges things like softball, weight watchers programs, and so on, all available and paid for by the firm. We have an ice cream guy, manicures, shoeshines, happy hours, and parlor games like pinball. It is wonderful that management sees the need to take a moment and says we need a time-out. It's all an avenue for people from other groups and floors to get together.

Why is this place so attractive to people? It's an equal balance between rapid skill (and career) development, niceness, and money.

Personalities who thrive at Mustang put all three on an even plane. There are no priorities among the three. If you don't do all three you lose people.

However, at the end of the day, none of these tactics is the message. Instead, the keys to success are the character, trust, and value system that are behind it.

So, what does all this say to you? Here are a few highlights of what it said to me:

It struck me that it was a mid-level employee, not the manager, who summed up the theory of the place as "good people management leads to longevity which leads to trust relationships with clients, which leads to more business." Would that all mid-level people understood that, believed that, and, what is most triumphant, believed that their management believed that.

You can't miss the references to fun, can you? Granted, these are marketing communications people, but is it too much of a stretch to think that lawyers, accountants, bankers, architects, and others want to have fun at work? How many managers go out of their way to create (and explicitly manage) a fun environment? Is it really generalizable that adding fun to discipline is a profit improvement tactic? These people think so, and so do I.

But the managers here are no pushovers. Listen again: "We take performance seriously. People get tired of other people who don't hold up their end of the deal. You either get the work done or you don't. You own it or not." Not a lot of wriggle-room there. It's clear that you can be (must be?) simultaneously tough and tender.

Don't miss the reference to "magnet people." Or the description "Our managers are amazingly brilliant people. They're smart, but human." Or the final quote: "The keys to success are the character, trust, and value system." Are you beginning to see a pattern here?

CHAPTER SEVEN

The Predictive Package

In this chapter, for the first time in our quantitative analysis, we stop looking at the survey questions one at a time, and start looking at them as an interrelated package. We now ask, "What package of questions are the best predictors of financial performance?"

To determine if there is a set of questions that could effectively predict an office's financial performance, a technique known as *stepwise regression analysis* was used. This method added and removed questions systematically, testing each time for explanatory power and statistical significance, to arrive at the set of questions that, taken together, best accounted for the variations in the financial performance index.

From the 74 questions originally asked, the result was nine key statements, which together "explain" over 50 percent of all variations in profit performance, in spite of big differences of country, size of practice, leverage and line of business.

The nine key statements are:

❑ Client satisfaction is a top priority at our firm.
❑ We have no room for those who put their personal agenda ahead of the interests of the clients or the office.
❑ Those who contribute the most to the overall success of the office are the most highly rewarded.

❏ Management gets the best work out of everybody in the office.

❏ Around here you are required, not just encouraged, to learn and develop new skills.

❏ We invest a significant amount of time in things that will pay off in the future.

❏ People within our office always treat others with respect.

❏ The quality of supervision on client projects is uniformly high.

❏ The quality of the professionals in our office is as high as can be expected.

We must stress that the list of nine items is, indeed, a package. It is the interactive combination of all nine that explains differences in profitability, not a simple addition of nine separate things.

So, let's look at the package in a little more depth.

Client satisfaction is a top priority at our firm.

No surprises here, which doesn't minimize its importance. Note from Appendix 2 that the employees' responses to this question varied quite a bit. In some places, apparently, there is real cynicism as to whether client satisfaction is a real priority. This is not a throwaway question.

We have no room for those who put their personal agenda ahead of the interests of the clients or the office.

Wow! Look how strongly this is stated. I actually stole the concept from Goldman Sachs's statement of values, along with some other questions in the survey. It's interesting (and probably not surprising) that at least one of Goldman's values turns out to be a profit predictor in a totally different set of businesses.

So, it turns out that true teamwork wins. Collaborative offices do better. Is anyone surprised?

Those who contribute the most to the overall success of the office are the most highly rewarded.

Well, I'm glad this one made it. Of course compensation is critical, and a nonnegotiable part of an excellence package. Note the language: It simply asks whether the employees think the right people are being rewarded. It does not speak to what that reward system should look like, except to point out that it specifies "the overall success of the office," which suggests that an individual incentive scheme would probably not meet this test.

Management gets the best work out of everybody in the office.

What does this one really mean? It says that everyone's working at his or her best. In other words, no one's cruising. This makes sense. If everyone else is really trying and performing at the peak of their capabilities, then it's easier for me to throw myself into my work, and find the energy, drive and discipline to really contribute.

If, on the other hand, this were not true, and some others in my office are not working at their best, then two things happen. First, it becomes clear that it's OK for me to cruise and just do my job, as others are doing, and, second, it becomes a little harder to find my own energy and drive if others are not showing it. It's clear why this one affects financial performance.

It suggests that management needs to be less tolerant, and ensure that everyone's working at his or her best. Notice, it doesn't say that everyone needs to be working at the same level. Only at their personal best.

Around here you are required, not just encouraged, to learn and develop new skills.

Another strong one. This statement, though phrased forcefully (softer options were available) is nothing more than a call for continuous self-improvement and lifelong learning. In a marketplace that is rapidly changing, it should be clear why this is a profit driver. What's not so clear is why so many offices (according to our data) do poorly on this one.

We invest a significant amount of time in things that will pay off in the future.

Again, there should be no surprises. If you think or perceive that management is betting on the future, it's a whole lot easier to throw yourself into your work and be energized by it. If, however, you think management fails this test, and isn't investing for the future, then why bother throwing yourself into things? Why not take care of today and leave it at that? It won't produce great financial performance, but, hey, if they don't believe in the future of this place, why should you?

People within our office always treat others with respect.

The wild card? I couldn't be more delighted that data and statistics prove that this is a profit driver, but I will confess I didn't predict it. So, who knew? When people feel respected they make more money for you! Gee, I wish this one were done better around the world. Look at the range on this question in Appendix 2; the numbers are scary. But also note how often this word "respect" comes up in our interviews with the superstar offices. Also note that this is not (just) about managers treating employees with respect; it's bigger than that. The statement says "People within our office always treat others with respect." That's all people, all the time. We're talking pervasive cultures here.

The quality of supervision on client projects is uniformly high.

How basic can you get? If you always supervise your clients' work well, you make money. This is news? Well, yes it is!

I've written about this a lot (see the introduction to my book *True Professionalism*), and provide an evaluation form to monitor this standard in my book *Managing the Professional Service Firm*. Most people understand that if you supervise projects well, you get a variety of benefits: lower turnover of staff, better work quality, better-trained people, more profitable projects, and so on. The trouble is that project leaders and "account supervisors" are busy people with many demands on their time (including demands from clients) and it is all too easy to fall into the trap of supervising with a style of "Here, do this. Catch me if you have any questions!"

Look at the data in Appendix 2, and see how many offices do this well! It may be obvious, but that doesn't mean it's consistently done well.

The quality of the professionals in our office is as high as can be expected.

A little repetitive of the statement about management getting the best out of everyone, but it's not quite the same. This one basically says we don't compromise standards in hiring, just to meet a capacity need. If you've been reading the case studies in this book, you will recognize that principle. You make money if you have high standards, and never compromise them. What a concept!

Putting It Together

So, what does this list of nine key variables mean? Are they the answer?

Not quite. An understanding of how regression works will shed some light on how we should interpret these nine statements.

First, note that it is a relatively balanced package representing a broad range of topics, from client focus through compensation, teamwork, project supervision, standards, and on to management's ability to get the best out of people.

This is no coincidence. Take, for example, the fact that "client service is a priority" is the only client focus variable included. Does that mean that the many other marketing, client relationship and client service questions were not important? No, it only means that once the computer program had accounted for the "client service priority" question, it looked for the next question that could explain variations in financial performance, *that the "client service priority" question had not already accounted for.*

Another way of saying this is to point out that most of the client focus questions were correlated with each other, and hence one could stand as a proxy for all. This does not minimize the central fact that the topic of client focus was the first variable the computer chose to "explain" differences in financial performance. It might look lonely on the page, but it's important. Very important!

The same logic, of course, applies to each of the other questions. Almost all of the questions in the list of nine have other similarly phrased questions in the survey. (This was done intentionally, to cross-validate the responses.) So, the question that says, in effect, "We have no room for individualists" is acting as a proxy for similar questions in the survey about teamwork and placing the client's interests first. One should not give too much emphasis to the fact that this question was chosen, rather than a similar one. It is the topic that is important, not the phrasing of the question.

One exception to this is that when given a choice between hard and soft questions ("We are team players" versus "We have no room for those who put their individual interests first"), the statistical technique consistently picked the harder, tougher version as being more predictive of profits.

A moment's reflection should immediately show why this would be so. The soft version of "We are kinda, sorta team players" is less likely to produce financial results than a statement that says "Absolutely we are team players, we don't accept anything else." In essence, we are talking about the difference between what you believe in ("please try") and what you actually execute ("we enforce this"). When it comes to making money, it's disciplined execution that counts, and good, thorough execution requires *strong* statements about the way the business is to be run.

Another statistical point is worth making. Look at the simple correlation (Appendix 5) of "People around here treat others with respect." If you looked at that correlation alone (which is quite low), you might not think this is a significant variable.

However, things that look relatively unimportant when examined in isolation can be powerful (at the margin) as an addition to the package. That's what stepwise regression looks for. If you didn't have client focus, good work supervision and high standards, then respect might not do much for you. But if you have those things, then adding a culture of respect, it turns out, does make a significant difference.

A final statistical note. You may notice that in our individual case studies, the things that a particular superstar office most excels at (the top ten things where it most outperforms the database) do not always include the nine items listed here. This is not a contradiction.

These nine items are a generalization of what "explains" differences in financial performance across *all* the offices and the *entire range* of performance. They represent a "best bet" as to what to focus on to improve profits and growth. They are not, however, the *only* way to do it. Most of our superstar offices did do well on these things, but did even better on some other employee attitudes: I chose only to present the top ten for each office. Remember, as we reported in chapter 3, the top 20 percent offices (financially) did better at virtually everything.

The nine items reported here represent a great place to get started.

CHAPTER EIGHT

Archipelago: A Case Study

Archipelago, one office of a much larger firm, is probably the most financially successful office in the database. Its financial performance was three times that of the average office, driven by outstanding margins and very rapid growth. The manager I talked with had recently been promoted, and was no longer in the same location as the staff that completed the survey. No staff were interviewed.

Here are the ten employee attitude scores, in descending order, where Archipelago most outperformed other offices (by 28 to 42 percent).

1. We have high-quality training opportunities to improve skills.
2. Management shows by their actions that employee training is important.
3. We regularly discuss our progress toward our strategic objectives, not just the financial goals.
4. Around here you are required, not just encouraged, to learn and develop new skills.
5. The management of our office always listens to our people.
6. We keep our people informed about what is happening in the office.
7. Management gets the best work out of everybody in the office.

8. Communication between the office's management and people at my level is very good.
9. Those who contribute the most to the overall success of the office are the most highly rewarded.
10. We invest a significant amount of time in things that will pay off in the future.

Here's the office head reflecting on the office's achievement:

How did we get these results? One reason is size. Small is good, since it is easier for a manager to make an impact on people.

Our principle is that you must be a team player. If you are a manager, you wash your own cup. It shows that you are not hierarchical. But you can't do it to be manipulative. People sense the sincerity. When you do it right, it works.

We start meetings on time even if everyone is not there. I give people grief when they are late. I point out that it is rude to others and it is disrespectful.

I get people to trust me by really caring about them and their development. If someone were thinking of leaving, and if it were right for him or her, I would encourage the person and even coach them to do so.

Why does that approach make money? Because all the rest don't leave as fast. You have disarmed them, and they believe that this place is a good place. When they do leave they feel good about the place. We have a strong alumni group. My posture is, "I won't let you go until you find an opportunity that is good enough for you."

I often dissuade people from leaving by telling them, "You are not done here" or "That new job is not the best opportunity for you." Or I may say "Bye! This is a good decision, I can't argue with it." People appreciate the truth especially when it is delivered with passion and they know you care about them.

People take criticism from me because they know I'm apolitical. Being superpolitical doesn't work here. I would not tolerate it. You have radar for that and try to weed out those that don't fit.

I really try to help my people. They believe my feedback. Most decisions I make have no particular benefit to me. I try to always do things for the greater good. It is my style. It wins for me.

I have learned that not everyone necessarily thinks like I do. So I try to think about what motivates each individual, especially given the generational differences. You've got to manage people in the way that works for each individual, not just how you like to manage. Being a good manager means being able to change your style to the type of person you are managing. But you must be careful because you don't want to be a chameleon. Just be adaptable.

Having like-minded people is important and makes everything easier. What am I looking for in a like-minded person? Someone who likes teamwork. No egomaniacs. Everyone has a voice. In trying to find the right people, I focus on energy and spirit. You have to ask, "What is their motivation? Why do they want to join us? What are the things that will help them to succeed? Who will be a good collaborator?" You have to weed out people who seem uptight on the job and who are concerned with rank.

We focus on good quality work, but we have fun along the way. We let people try new things. We give them a long rope. If you are consistent in what you expect, people will usually select themselves out. But as a manager you must be consistent with your values and expectations.

I'm a good listener. Not only to other people but I also listen to my gut. If I feel uncomfortable it is for a reason, and I pay attention to that. Of all my effort to energize people, way over 50 percent is one-on-one. Most impact and change occurs when management is one-on-one. All group stuff is informational. It is the hygiene.

I try to keep a balance among focusing on my people, my clients and the finances. I can do all three at once, whereas many managers can only handle one. I spend about 50 percent of my time with my people, 30 percent with the clients and 20 percent on the finances. In larger offices, it will probably be 60 to 70 percent with people, 10 percent with clients and 10 to 20 percent on finances. I probably would have liked to spend more time with clients. But it is more important that my people learn how to spend time with the clients.

We give our employees a sense of pride in shooting high. This is an ambitious, high, stretch-goal kind of place. We showcase what good work is. We show people the difference between good work and good-enough work.

What do I do to get people to believe the right people are rewarded? More good jobs are given to better workers. I give them more diversified work or work with different opportunities giving them more stimulating things.

I announce pay decisions one-on-one, explaining to people why they got what they got. Timeliness is important. How you deliver things, your message. The wrapper you put your message in is important.

We have concrete yearly reviews but spot bonuses are extra for a job well done. I think the process of compensation setting is being managed well. The message is that it is not about the money. A formal raise is given on your anniversary date with the firm. Senior people's reviews are done quarterly. This forces a management leadership discussion.

Around here you are required to learn new skills. This means that somebody who wants a job and not a career would not be tolerated. Work tasks are constantly changing and a huge amount of judgment is required even at a junior level. The demand to keep learning new things is made palatable because we actively work at helping people dream, and because it is fun. If you have accepted a new challenge and overcome an obstacle you have learned something and it's fun. If you don't find that fun, you're not for us.

Why doesn't this happen everywhere? I suspect it is because other managers haven't had good experiences themselves with role models. Role models are important; they are the essence. Values of right or wrong must be displayed. You need boosters, people who will say, "You can do it, you can do it!"

Is there anything we did differently in dealing with clients that led to our good financial and attitude results? If we get a sense that we can't care about this client, we won't propose. If we get a sense that the client can't hold up their end of the relationship, or that it will be a boring account, we won't take it. You have to remember that we have good, cool people working for us and we can't put them into a dull situation. It won't work. We push back with clients who don't treat us well. We don't tolerate them. Our people are what are important.

We believe that you should never propose on stuff you can't care about. It won't be good work. If your heart is not in it, you won't be supersuccessful, which will hurt your reputation. We make money by succeeding in client relationships, and you can't do that if you don't care. If times weren't good, would we take a freak client? No. You don't make a wrong decision to hit a short-term financial goal.

It is harder to sustain this practice when you are small because you have a more immediate relationship with the money. In a larger organization you can absorb a few bad jobs and hide them in a larger volume of successes.

One thing I am working on now is sustaining the one-on-one culture in a larger multilocation firm. I'm trying to get all the office managers to share my point of view, but not by preaching at them. People learn by the example you give them. You set the tone and they take it back to their offices.

We prefer to promote our managers from within. Eighty percent of everything is hiring the right person. If they have 80 percent of the right core values, and if you model and reinforce them, they'll work out. We do people management training twice a year. People come from all offices. We also conduct twice-yearly firmwide meetings of all office managers where we feed off each other.

I visit all the offices regularly and try to meet all the employees. In my first six months, I must have spent time with at least one-half of the four hundred staff in our firm on a one-on-one basis.

All firms say the same things, but they don't all live what they say. The main management system here is that we live up to our values.

The real issue is the willingness to bet on long-term measures of many months, not just short-term expediency. You can't afford to get stampeded.

If we had to make a choice of "hit budget for a month" or "cancel training" what would we do? First, we'd try to be creative to see if we could, say, spend less on the training to get the same training benefit. If we couldn't do that, we wouldn't cancel the training. We'd bet on the long-term result.

We do use some creativity. We use whatever accounting leeway we have to build up cushions from good months, to give ourselves some insurance. We spend a lot of time identifying trends before they overtake us. If we foresee a downside coming, we take steps to counteract the problem before it actually occurs. That makes a large number of tradeoffs go away. But ultimately, we do what is right long-term for the client and for our employees.

Part of the reason we feel strongly about our culture is we have had it a long time. We have always operated this way. Once you create a momentum in the right direction, the easier it is. The more you focus on making money, the harder it is to do. You won't make same decisions if you just focus exclusively on money. Culture is important.

What was interesting to you here? I found everything this impressive person had to say fascinating, particularly given her track record. These things in particular stick out for me:

❑ Most decisions I make have no particular benefit to me. I try to always do things for the greater good.

❑ I probably would have liked to spend more time with clients. But it is more important that my people learn how to spend time with the clients.

❑ Most impact and change occurs when management is one-on-one.

❑ You don't make a wrong decision to hit a short-term financial goal.

These are simple, powerful statements of a clear philosophy about the role of a manager. And what's more impressive, she actually lives them! How rare to see someone with the courage of her convictions!

CHAPTER NINE

The Path to Performance

Warning! This chapter's a little bit complex, but very, very important. To encourage you to make the effort with this chapter, let me tell you, right up front, one of the conclusions you'll see reported here.

It turns out that we can *prove* that if an average office increased its performance by going from an average of "somewhat agree" to "agree" on the staff's rating of quality and client relationships, this would *cause* a doubling of its financial performance! That's right, cause. We will also show, specifically, what causes ratings of quality and client relationships to improve.

Although I obtained a master's degree in mathematical statistics thirty years ago, it turns out they've made a few advances since then. (Surprise!) The approach used in this chapter is known as *structural equation modeling.* It was new to me, and it took me a while to get my mind around it. But it was worth the effort, because what is presented here is, I think, truly profound. I've tried my best to make it accessible to the general reader, but it still may take a bit of concentrated attention! (A description of the methodology is given in Appendix 7.)

Correlation calculations (such as those used in chapter 5) check to see whether two things tend, on average, to move together (like height and weight). However, structural equation modeling checks to see if one of those things (say, extra height) can be said to *cause* the other (extra weight). If causality can be found, it estimates how much of weight change can be said to be caused by differences in height. (Not enough, regrettably. It seems diet and exercise also have something to do with it, alas!)

The technique is complex, so rather than use the 74 questions, I restricted attention to the nine factors we have been using, which, it will be recalled, are the result of combining the scores of a number of individual questions (Appendix 3).

Rather than explain the workings of the technique I'll jump straight to the results, which are shown in Figure 7–1. It's less complicated than it looks. Start by ignoring the numbers in the diagram, and focus on the solid and dotted lines. Every time you see a solid line on this diagram, it means that a statistically significant "causal link" has been established from the data. (All "nonsignificant" links were removed.) The dotted lines (which have an "r-squared" number rather than a "b") show relationships where correlation exists, but causality has not been established.

By almost any formal criterion developed by the scholars, the proposed model shown in Figure 7–1 is a good statistical fit to the data (Appendix 7). Let's analyze this complex diagram, step by step, starting at the top with financial performance.

As may be seen, one factor has a *direct* causal relationship with financial performance, and that is our measure of quality and client relationships. Here are the individual questions that make up that factor:

❏ We make our clients feel as if they're important to us.
❏ We keep clients informed on issues affecting their business.
❏ We have a real commitment to high levels of client service, and tolerate nothing else.
❏ Client satisfaction is a top priority at our firm.
❏ The quality of work performed for clients by my group is consistently high.
❏ We are extremely good at building long-term client relationships.

Figure 7–1: The Causal Model

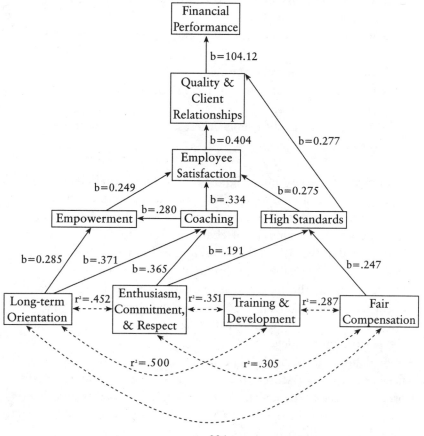

❏ The quality of service delivered to clients by my group is consistently high.

❏ Most people in our office do "whatever it takes" to do a good job for their clients.

❏ We do a good job of resolving client problems when they occur.

❏ We listen well to what the client has to say.

❏ We have a real commitment to high-quality work, and tolerate nothing less.

❏ We always place the clients' interests first, ahead of those of the office.

Conventional wisdom is right. Quality and client relationships drive profits. However, we can now provide a concrete estimate of how big this effect is. The size of the "b" score along the arrows in the diagram is the amount of change in the caused variable (the pointed end of the arrow) that would result from a one-unit change in the "causing" variable (the blunt end of the arrow.)

According to the diagram, a one-unit increase in quality and client relationships (from, say, 4.0-somewhat agree to 5.0-agree) on our 6-point scale would cause a 104.12 point increase in the financial performance index.

By definition, the financial performance index of the average office in our database scores 100 (it's an index). So, by going from an office average of "somewhat agree" to "agree" on quality and client relationships (in the eyes of staff) the average office would more than double its financial performance!

This is *really* strong stuff!

But What Drives Quality and Client Relationships?

We saw the power of quality and client relationships in chapter 5, when we examined correlations. We asked then, "But what drives quality and client relationships?"

We now have some answers. As Figure 7–1 shows, two factors

have a *direct* causal effect on quality and client relationships. These are high standards and employee satisfaction.

For the record, here are the component questions of the employee satisfaction factor as they were defined in Appendix 3.

- ❏ I am highly satisfied with my job.
- ❏ I get a great sense of accomplishment from my work.
- ❏ The overwhelming majority of the work I'm given is challenging rather than repetitive.
- ❏ I am committed to this firm as a career opportunity.

Raising employee satisfaction (i.e., these four questions) by 1 point on our 6-point scale (again we'll use the example of from "somewhat agree" to "agree") would improve the score on quality and client relationships by 0.4 (which is about a 10 to 15 percent improvement in most cases). This, in turn, would raise the financial performance index by (0.404 times 104.12) or 42.06.

Let's say that again, in reasonably plain English. We have *strong* evidence that a 10 to 15 percent increase in the scores given by employees to the elements of employee satisfaction will cause a 42.06 point increase in financial performance (or 42.06 percent for an average office.)

Let's say it one last time. Improve your office average by about 10 to 15 percent on the rating of these four items by your staff, and it will *cause* a 42 percent improvement in financial performance, including both profitability and growth.

What about improving high standards? Here are the elements that make up that factor:

- ❏ The quality of the professionals in our office is as high as can be expected.
- ❏ Poor performance is not tolerated here.
- ❏ This is a very demanding place to work.
- ❏ When necessary, people put the needs of the office ahead of their own.

❑ We have a strong culture. If you don't fit in, you won't make it here.

From our diagram, we can conclude that a one-point change in high standards would have two immediate consequences. First, employee satisfaction will increase by 0.275 units, because of the direct arrow to that factor.

Secondly, the score for quality and client relationships will be *directly* increased by 0.277 as well. (It is a coincidence that the size of these two effects is similar.)

Combining these two effects, we can calculate that if the average office with a high-standards score of "somewhat agree" could raise its performance to "agree" (or any other one-point change such as from "agree" to "strongly agree"), its financial performance would rise from 100 (the average office) to 140.4, a 40 percent improvement.

Not too shabby! And we have proof! (Well, not proof. The precise way to say it is that the data are consistent with this conclusion. Karl Popper, the eminent philosopher of science, argued that nothing could ever be proven; you could only say that something has not yet been refuted. Still, what we've got here is not bad, even by his standards!)

Table 7–1 shows a summary table of what a one-point increase in each of the factors (with causal links) would cause in financial performance (if everything else stays the same).

Remember, these are not additive. You can't just add up the column above and hope to triple profits by obtaining a one-point increase on all elements (although it might work out that way if you really did that well!)

What's the significance of the fact that the training and development factor has no causal links? Does that mean it's not important? After all, we have already seen that some of our superstar offices do particularly well at this.

It absolutely doesn't mean that training is unimportant. It means

Table 7–1: Effect of a 1-Point Improvement in the Factor Score on Financial Performance

Factor	Effect of a 1-Point Increase
Quality and client relationships	104.12
Employee satisfaction	42.06
High standards	40.40
Coaching	16.98
Commitment, enthusiasm, and respect	13.92
Empowerment	10.47
Fair compensation	9.98
Long-term orientation	9.28

we could not prove *causality* with the (tough) level of statistical certainty required by the technique employed.

Look at it this way. Training is influential, since it is correlated with many things. But by itself, it has few *direct, independent* consequences. If you tried to improve an office through training alone, it would probably have little impact. This is unlike some of our other factors, which do have a causal impact independent of what else is going on. Training and development can be part of the solution, but they are not the solution in themselves. It doesn't say don't do training; it says don't do only training and nothing else.

As may be seen, there are links of correlation between a number of the factors (shown by dotted arrows), showing that they are interrelated (they tend to move together), and these correlations are statistically significant. Only those links that passed the harder test of causality show up as solid lines in the diagram.

The label "r-squared" on the dotted links can be interpreted as follows. Examine the label "r-squared equals 0.45" on the link between long-term orientation and enthusiasm, commitment and respect. This means that 45 percent of the variation in one of these variables can be explained by variations in the other. In other words, they tend to move in synchronization. Not completely, but quite a lot. Employees who rate one highly tend to rate the other highly, too.

So where are we? Perhaps for the first time, we can now actually look at the profit implications of various managerial and policy decisions in a rigorous way. We are now in a position to suggest to managers precisely where they should focus their attention.

Is it easy? No! But we now know precisely what needs to be done. Not surprisingly, almost every aspect of employee attitudes and culture is involved in some way, some directly and some indirectly. But we have solid evidence of what the right path looks like. In simplified form, this is what we have shown:

- ❑ Financial performance is driven by quality and client relationships.
- ❑ Quality and client relationships are driven by employee satisfaction.
- ❑ Employee satisfaction is driven by high standards, coaching and empowerment.
- ❑ High standards are driven by fair compensation and commitment, enthusiasm, and respect.
- ❑ Coaching is driven by long-term orientation and commitment, enthusiasm, and respect.
- ❑ Empowerment is driven by long-term orientation.

Now, there's a litany worth posting on the wall!

CHAPTER TEN

Tigrette: A Case Study

Tigrette, a 300-person marketing consulting firm, achieved a financial performance index 73 percent above the norm, driven by superb margins and a growth rate in profit which was double the norm. The ten aspects of employee attitude where it most outperformed other offices were (in descending order):

1. We have high-quality training opportunities to improve skills.
2. Enthusiasm and morale around here have never been higher.
3. I am actively helped with my personal development.
4. This place has done a good job of providing the training I've needed to do my job well.
5. Management shows by their actions that employee training is important.
6. Considering the office as a whole, the compensation system is managed equitably and fairly.
7. We are extremely good at building long-term client relationships.
8. Management of our office is successful in fostering commitment and loyalty.
9. There is more opportunity to move ahead rapidly here than is possible at most other places.

10. We regularly discuss the results of client satisfaction feedback.

Here's Tigrette's CEO:

We let our people run their own businesses and do their own thinking. As long as it is on target we let it go. We are supportive all the way. We concentrate on positive things and don't emphasize the negative. Most importantly, we don't make last minute changes in their work before it goes to the client. We back our people up.

We do get involved early in projects. We watch the pulse of things, so there is no need to come in at the last minute and make huge changes causing disruption. To most people, last-minute changes are a big thing and they scare people.

We believe in keeping a level emotional keel. If we made a hiring mistake and found we had someone who yelled and screamed, we would fire that person if he or she couldn't be coached into good behavior. We actually have a special training course on anger management.

In service businesses, clients can be difficult. Some of our staff, of course, can manage that, but many become uncomfortable. So, to compensate, we try to make this as nice a workplace as we can. The nicer it is at work, the better it is for the firm.

We look for a cooperative spirit in our people, a dedication to the goal as a team, and a service mentality. We look for an attitude that is nonargumentative. We want people who can be encouraged to raise their own ideas, but know when to back off.

We also find success by moving people from team to team. We watch the chemistry and how people work together and how the client reacts to them. We encourage cross-team collaboration. Some people, although not formally involved with a project, may offer to help and add significant impact. That gets remembered. We like to develop our own people and promote from within.

Financial incentives play a part in achieving high morale because of our pension plan where people can get the maximum contribution. Most places don't give everyone the ability to get the highest percentage allowed by law. Through our cash bonus plan (an unusual opportunity) everyone qualifies to be recognized. Everyone feels they have a shot at the piece of the action. But if you don't perform you get zip; it is purely discretionary.

We have everyone sign a confidentiality statement regarding compensation and bonuses, so no one else knows what another person gets. This agreement is taken seriously and everyone knows that management is willing to enforce it.

Good training also keeps morale high. We also consistently thank people for a job well done and give them a pat on back at the time it happens. We have an open-door policy at the firm. Everyone is approachable. In fact, our culture is such that you are not allowed not to be approachable.

Enthusiasm is also high because of our parties, newsletters, and such things. They make everyone feel more like a team. Off-site events may not be crucial, but they support the culture. The low departure and high return rate of employees prove this.

People feel they are actively helped with their personal development. We have a "Lunch and Learn" series of mini-workshops. We have courses. We pay for outside courses that people can select themselves, with full tuition reimbursement. We also have managerial training for managers at all levels.

There is no fixed schedule of training. People are supposed to take one or two outside courses a year as part of their development. People are free to find their own courses and study that which they enjoy or want to learn about.

This is all very expensive but we are convinced that spending the money makes sense. If we didn't do it, the consequences would be faster turnover and a lower quality of work. We have also found that the interaction of people on our courses leads to better interpersonal skills. We also do sensitivity training and team building exercises.

We don't track the percentage of our fees that we spend on training. We look at the big picture. If we can afford it and think it will be good, we try it. Of all our training about 80 percent is about personal development and only 20 percent is technical training.

For example, we offer a popular course on handling conflicts. No one ever teaches you in school how to handle conflict, yet it's a part of everybody's life, senior and junior.

How do we foster commitment and loyalty? We don't complicate our people's working lives by getting involved in their day-to-day activities. We know *who* each person is. We know their quirks and their problems, both personally and professionally. We try to do personal things personally for them. For example, we recently wrote a check for someone who was closing on a house and whose bank couldn't get her the money in time.

This type of spirit, attitude, willingness is the culture, top to bottom. We insist that our staff operate this way. Our culture is getting people to behave the right sort of way toward their fellow workers as well as to clients.

To get people to operate in this style, we try to hire people who have this innate in their personality. If they aren't going to fit into our culture, they don't belong here. When hiring we may call their previous or existing clients or someone else who knows them to ask about their people skills.

The culture stresses that there is no "behind closed doors" behavior by managers. There is no executive-floor attitude. All managers are integrated. We are expected to know how each other's life is going and what we are doing, again, both personally and professionally.

People make their own decisions. Our philosophy is: "You will not get penalized for doing something, only for doing nothing." When a mistake is made, our attitude is "move on and don't criticize." Emphasize the positive. We don't criticize and penalize like other firms do.

When interviewing people (as well as on a daily basis in the workplace) we inform people and are clear about our plans, our goals and objectives. It builds great trust when they see at the end of the year that we deliver on our promise.

Although we have policies and procedures, we use great flexibility. For example, we have no strict policy on vacations. We are willing to give time off (that doesn't count against vacation time) if it is needed for personal reasons or for a job well done. There is no "nine-to-five" mentality. Of course, we have normal hours, but if someone stays late they aren't expected in first thing next day.

We had a burned-out team last year that had worked their backs off. As recognition we gave them a special bonus in addition to encouraging them to take paid time off. We try to prove that management cares, that the staff are people and not just bodies to burn out.

Another thing we do is to arrange special dinners or give free tickets. Anyone can receive such an appreciation. From the janitor on up, management puts itself in an employee's shoes and knows what that employee is going through.

We don't overmanage, but everyone knows and respects the need to focus on client needs. You present your idea, but at some point, if the client isn't willing, you have to do what the client wants. Our people embrace the team effort to keep the client happy. We have no dictatorship on teams.

We have a strong track record of building long-term client relationships. We make it our business to know all the departments within our clients, not just the ones we happen to be working with today. We work at client relations by trying to do fun things with them. All levels of people get tickets and perks.

Success in professional services is about personality synchronization, finding the right chemistry between provider and client executive. We encourage all of our employees to be involved at *all* levels of the client organization.

You learn this kind of involvement by doing it together with those who are more senior than you. If someone at the junior level is not getting it, they will receive a message that "socializing" needs to be done. It must be a continual process for everyone. People know that involving themselves with clients is part of their performance review.

Middle-Level Group

Now let's hear from a middle-level group at this firm:

What's distinctive about this place is sensitivity to what staff is going through. We middle-level managers have the freedom to do what we have to do in order to improve morale. For example, if everyone is busy on a project, a manager can feel free to bring in lunch for all at the firm's expense. We don't have to get an okay or permission to do so. We have the freedom to make decisions.

The most important thing is that everyone knows that the firm will support you, and they will recognize what's happening and not be afraid to reward. We went through a particularly hard time on a project and the firm threw a big party to console us and celebrate a great effort.

People like what they do here. People pitch in because they know the firm, and our co-workers are good to us. Everyone feels pride and ownership for the firm and for what they do. We know the firm takes care of us. We have fun doing what we do.

In the interviewing process if you get the feeling that someone won't fit in, then he or she doesn't get hired, no matter what that person's technical ability may be. Our rule is "Talent doesn't outweigh personality."

If someone, in any role, were not nice, that person would be counseled and then fired if the counseling didn't work. It's happened. We don't tolerate anyone who is abusive. There is no management through intimidation here. No "I'm the boss" attitude. No toleration of undermining people. Individualists don't last. It's a matter of culture, not systems.

On the other hand, we do tolerate a lot from clients. But inside the firm, there is no lack of consideration for any person. Everyone's voice is appreciated and heard. You can speak out no matter what your title is. Management (and everyone else) listens.

Very little comes down from management around here. Most goes up. We emphasize managing up. People are held accountable and most fulfill their responsibilities. Nothing festers.

People get to do what they want to do. Personal development goes ahead of profits. (This is a shift since the people crisis hit.) It is more important to get the right people than worry about the financial margin of what the employee will cost.

Because this firm knows its people and its people know its clients, there is a natural sense of who goes where. Once a year we each have a formal sitdown with management, one-on-one, and talk about what we like to do and what we want to work on. We have both a self-evaluation and a performance appraisal.

That the firm spends money on training is very important. If we don't educate ourselves, we can't educate the client. Everyone is encouraged to take two courses per year and is allowed to choose what they want.

On-the-job learning here is a baptism of fire. People get tossed into jobs and training becomes on the job. There are formal on-site as well as off-site training programs. Training participation is considered very important. Here if a person says, "I can't make the seminar because of a client conflict," management is very apt to call the client and say, "My person needs to do this. Can I fill in or make other arrangements?" And usually the client understands.

Many people who leave here ask to come back. They say, "It was not as nice at the other place. Management there is not as involved or interested." Here we genuinely care about people. And the benefits are good! Here we recognize that work life and home life need to balance.

We have profit sharing. Everyone gets rewarded the same percentage, and here they go for the maximum allowed by law. Everyone gets to participate and have a shot at a cash bonus, based on performance. This has nothing to do with the annual review and the raise that comes with that. That is the performance appraisal system, which is performed annually, a must. A yearly raise is usually the result, but almost always with a concrete action plan to improve. If you come up with a good idea that gets used, you get a gift certificate.

Top management is transparent, not opaque. They live the message of their cult. Respect for other people is a key part of this firm, inside and outside. We are good at building client relationships. We do our homework, trying to bring new things to the client on a regular basis. We are not afraid to give our opinions. We take the time and make the effort to learn about our clients and to find out about them personally.

We focus on long-term, in-depth relationships with clients. Our clients look to us as a resource. We make it our business to know both their past and present situation. We'll spend money to speak with consultants specializing in our client's field to find out what is going on with the industry and organization.

You don't need top management approval to do it here, either. This firm spends money on building teams. We have lots of non-work-related activities with everyone here (and with clients) to get to know each other as people. For example, we gave one of our client's people a baby shower.

We care. We have a can-do attitude. "Can't" is not part of our vocabulary. We are very careful never to talk down to clients. Or to anyone else for that matter.

Firms that stress niceness find that it helps to earn trust and also allows you to say "No" to the client when it is appropriate. What we mean by being nice is a set of skills, including diplomacy, courtesy, professionalism and no superficiality. We have a sense of who is and who is not a Tigrette person. Our philosophy is "If you wouldn't want them over to your house for lunch, don't hire them!"

Are there lessons of particular significance here? Here are a few of mine:

I love this sentence: "Talent doesn't outweigh personality." Boy, could a few of my clients take that one to heart! Or this one: "Success in professional services is about personality synchronization." Apart from paying them well and giving them a share of the profits, this firm works hard at treating people, employees and clients, as individuals, and ensuring they are compatible. These people have built their success on an understanding of how to build relationships, a single mentality which is then applied to both clients and employees.

CHAPTER ELEVEN

Firm or Office? What's Driving Things?

Is an organization's culture defined at the firm or office level? This simple question highlights a fundamental issue we alluded to earlier, the role of the individual manager within the firm.

There is no question, at least in this database, that the individual office performance strongly outweighs any firmwide effect. (Firmwide differences in our survey, as we shall see, do exist, but they are less strong than those of the individual offices.)

Take, for example, one firm in our study that has 14 offices. Table 11–1 shows the scores on the nine factors of the best and worst performing offices within that firm, compared to their firmwide average.

These are huge percentage swings, compared to the relatively modest 5 to 10 percent improvements that we saw (in chapter 3) distinguished the most successful offices from the rest of the pack. Compared to these *"within* firm" differences, the differences *between* companies on their aggregate results tend to pale into insignificance.

This was tested by examining where the "between-firm" averages *were* big enough to be statistically significant. We did find some areas of small, but systematic, differences between firms.

Here are the ten items that showed the *most* statistically significant differences between *firm* averages:

Table 11–1: How the Best- and Worst-Performing Offices at One Firm Compared to Firmwide Averages

Factor	Percent that Worst Performing Office scored compared to firmwide average	Percent that Best Performing Office scored compared to firmwide average
Commitment, enthusiasm and respect	−21	+13
Training and development	−19	+11
Coaching	−18	+11
Long-term orientation	−15	+8
Empowerment	−14	+15
Employee satisfaction	−13	+9
Fair compensation	−11	+17
Quality and client relationships	−9	+5
High standards	−8	+3

1. We have high-quality training opportunities to improve skills.
2. Management shows by their actions that employee training is important.
3. This place has done a good job of providing the training I've needed to do my job well.

4. We have a strong culture. If you don't fit in, you won't make it here.
5. This is a very demanding place to work.
6. The overwhelming majority of the work I'm given is challenging rather than repetitive.
7. There are real opportunities here for meaningful career and professional advancement.
8. The quality of the professionals in our office is as high as can be expected.
9. We are extremely good at building long-term client relationships.
10. In this office we set and enforce very high standards for performance.

Note that only some of these questions (where firms, as firms, differ most) appear in our previous list of key profit drivers. Questions 8, 9 and 10 are key profit drivers, but our analysis in previous chapters gives a lesser role to questions 1 through 7.

Compare that list to the ten questions with the *least* significant differences between firms:

1. Considering my contribution, I think I am paid fairly compared to others in the office.
2. Considering the office as a whole, the compensation system is managed equitably and fairly.
3. I am highly satisfied with my job.
4. I get a great sense of accomplishment from my work.
5. Poor performance is not tolerated here.
6. Communication between the office's management and people at my level is very good.
7. I am a member of a well-functioning team.
8. We do a good job of delegating work to the appropriate level.
9. I often express my views on issues important to me, even when I know that others will disagree.

10. The amount of work I have keeps me challenged, but not overwhelmed.

In contrast to the previous list, most of these questions *are* in the key profit drivers (with the possible exception of question 6 on communication.) Firms do differ at the firmwide level, but not predominantly on the things that matter most!

Forty percent of the survey questions had a statistically significant variance between firms. The rest did not, revealing that differences in culture, management practices and values mostly rest at the level of the individual office, not the firm.

Examining the nine factors, we find that the most important factor (as shown by our causal modeling in chapter 9), quality and client relationships, shows barely significant differences between firms. Similarly, employee satisfaction, fair compensation, empowerment, and commitment, enthusiasm and respect are *not* significantly different at the firm level.

It needs to be stressed that it could have been possible for firmwide effects to occur. If a firm had a sufficiently enforced set of firmwide values that all of their offices (and everyone within them) *had to* observe, then we would have seen common patterns of behavior (and similar survey results) across all locations of the firm.

That, however, is not what we are seeing. Many firms (including a number in this database) have well-articulated (and entirely sensible) values, principles and management philosophies at the firm level. What they do not have, according to our data, is any mechanism to ensure that these are operational and consistently observed across the firm. They lack *enforcement* of what they say they believe in.

Clearly, managers of individual offices have a great deal of leverage in building the type of office environment they desire. Whatever is intended by firmwide management, the individual local manager is disproportionately influential in creating the local culture.

What does this mean? If you believe that behavior in firms is largely explainable by the fact that firms are composed exclusively of people, and particular kinds of people at that, it is hardly surprising that *personal* connections matter most to them: individual client connections and individual peer connections. Loyalty is rarely loyalty to the firm; it is loyalty to particular people.

Managerial influence is not achieved by themes, or issues, or mandates, or even visions. It is achieved, if at all, by individual people. Thus the success of these characteristics at the office level, not the firm level, makes perfect sense.

The success of a business is a matter of choosing the right managers, not choosing the right corporate policies. A huge amount of time is spent worrying about and developing corporate strategies, missions, policies and practices. The amount of time spent thinking about, screening for and appointing the best managers pales in comparison. Maybe it's time for firms to switch their attention to what really counts.

This does not mean that there is no role for firmwide missions, values, principles and standards. It does mean that that firms need to have mechanisms to ensure that these things are being applied everywhere. In turn, this usually means that the local (or business unit) managers that are selected are prepared to be the shining embodiment of those values. Rather than selecting for business development skills, financial acumen or technical excellence, firms need to choose managers who *really* know how to manage!

CHAPTER TWELVE

Mortimer Ransford: A Case Study

Mortimer Ransford is a 200-person firm specializing in direct marketing, client-loyalty programs, consumer and trade promotions, and marketing strategy and communications. In eighteen months, it doubled its revenues and margins. Here's Colin Ransford, CEO of Mortimer Ransford:

We really believe that *chasing* money is not what *makes* you money. We believe that if you have the right client base, the right people with the right attitudes, and the right systems, the money will follow. If all you do is worry about the last ten cents on every deal, you won't get anywhere.

We made a big decision two years ago, turning down (for the first time) a potentially lucrative opportunity, because it was really boring work. We asked, "Is this what our life has come to, pitching for this kind of work?" On the same grounds, we resigned one of our largest accounts, one we had worked on for four years, and one that had consistently earned us strong revenues. When we first started on the account, it was exactly the type of work we wanted. However, over time we became the "bottom of the food chain" for this client.

We didn't like working that way, and we deserved a lot better. The work was neither intellectually challenging nor strategically satisfying, and we knew that at some point the client would spot our boredom, because we could only cover it up for so long.

So, we decided we would walk away. It's easy firing a small client, but this was huge! We stopped being nervous about two weeks after we dropped this client, because we realized that resigning that business was the best thing we'd ever done. In fact it was so obvious that we asked ourselves why we hadn't done it earlier.

There were immediate, tangible benefits from this. We sent a strong signal to our staff that the guys at the top were not afraid to make the difficult decisions, and that we were in touch with the quality of all of the firm's accounts. And if the top guy walked away from such a large account because of the nature of the work, the chances of any staff member getting stuck on a boring project in the future suddenly got a lot slimmer.

It gave a sense of renewal to our people. We'd thought we were doing well by working on rather dull, easy-to-turn-around projects that make us reasonable money. But that work prevented our really good people from being able to develop much more interesting client opportunities, ones that they personally would get a much bigger kick from, and ones that would dramatically improve the firm's performance.

We've pitched eighteen to twenty times during the last twelve months, and we have turned down at least twelve serious pitches during that time. This might sound counterintuitive, but we find that whenever we turn down a brief, we nearly always discover an upside. What happens is that by turning down major client work, which is generally unheard of in this sector, you become sought after. Our reputation has grown and our revenues have gone through the roof.

I'm not saying that only great creative projects matter. Nor only intellectual stimulation. Obviously, nor only money. We need a balance of all three, a balance where our staff gets the great work, our clients get great work from us, and we make lots of money.

We have certain nonnegotiable cultural minimums. They are difficult to write down because we don't think about them, we just live them. Things like disrespect for titles and hierarchy, and an acute apathy for accepting conventional wisdom in every facet of the business. Our open plan for offices, we hope, is in parallel with and reinforces our open-plan thought process, and open-plan lack of politics.

Every Friday afternoon we all get together and review the week. Someone always wins a prize for making the week's best nonfinancial contribution to the firm. It's a transitional downtime, when people stop being the writer or the account handler or the data planner, and become the person that they are.

We recognize that we need to be busy, interesting, active, diverse, human beings. We recognize that we are something different when we walk out the door for the weekend, and because of that, when we walk back in through the door, we bring more with us. This is very touchy-feely, which is why we've never written it down.

We encourage a certain thought process in our people. We want them to ask themselves questions such as, "Can I get along with people at *all* levels? Do I contribute to clients of the office that I'm *not responsible* for looking after? Although I haven't been asked, and I don't really need to, will I turn up for that other team's brainstorming session because I *want* to?"

Our objective is to create an increasingly balanced scorecard for the firm, taking into account not only financial results but also employee development and client satisfaction. To date, we have done quite a good job of creating a customized version of this. We now have several initiatives in place to continue strengthening the employee-loyalty piece of the scorecard.

We have a high-profile internal creative award, the winning team being chosen by expert external judges. This happens every three months and the winners get their work exhibited around the firm. Everyone involved with the account shares the glory.

We have a very active program of cross-functional information sharing, using briefs, e-mails, lunches, whatever. We have an in-house satirical magazine that we publish every quarter. We have just started a rolling program of staff-satisfaction surveys, which we have written in a style that fits our self-deprecating culture.

Most importantly, we've appointed a very senior account han-

dler to manage the whole balanced-scorecard process. He personally represents the values we'd like everyone in the firm to live. He's
our "culture cop" and his appointment sent another strong message
to the firm that we're serious about delivering the balanced-
scorecard model.

We've done some client surveys but it's not yet a regular process.
I want our staff reviews to be based significantly, but not exclusively, on client feedback. I then want to attempt to *link* client and
employee satisfaction. It would allow mid-level account handlers
to be able to take true ownership of the health of client relationships. At the moment, they tend to duck when the bullets start firing. I think it would be a very good device to force us to grow up
quickly.

We plan to institutionalize meetings with clients every three or
six months to talk about the health of our relationship. This will
form the basis of ongoing fee negotiation as well. We'll talk about
our people working on the account and how the client feels they're
doing. We'll talk about how much time we're spending on the account, and whether the client feels we're overpaid, underpaid, or
fairly paid.

These meetings can serve as a precontract contract negotiation,
as a health check, and as a way to get objective feedback on how
well the account handler is doing. The account handler will know
the meeting is taking place, but will not be a part of the meeting; we
will tell the account handlers the results of the meeting in an open
dialogue. Most importantly, we will be able to determine how the
client feels about our work and our service. The results will then
have a positive or negative effect on our people's performance reviews, and may or may not impact their salaries and/or bonuses.

I need the staff to feel this is a really good idea. I want to use this
feedback loop as an intuitive management tool that has an upside
for all parties. This will also strengthen the client-loyalty piece of
our scorecard.

We decided management couldn't make the balanced scorecard
happen ourselves; we just wouldn't have the time. So we needed

someone to make sure the theory turned into practice. This person could become the living embodiment of the balanced scorecard.

We happened to have an ideal candidate in the person of Arthur Orbach, who had been with us for several years as a senior account handler. He had always been interested in, and attuned to, cultural issues, specifically the "what will it take to make this a great place to work?" issue.

So we said, "Arthur, we don't know the answers, but we expect you to find them for us! We'll want some deliverables, not just a party every two months, but more solid stuff." And we agreed we should follow the sequence: happy staff equals happy clients equals more profit. Other than that there were no rules.

Here's Arthur Orbach's side of the story:

What Colin was proposing to me was fine in theory, but I needed to feel this job would have commercial teeth. Colin is not the sentimental sort; if he doesn't think an idea has business logic, he trashes it. This was reassuring, as I knew he wouldn't try to sell me something he thought was tree-hugging, hippie nonsense.

If my mandate was to make the place great, there were no limits. Everything I did would be good because it would be something that other firms were probably not getting around to doing. We spent a long time agreeing what results would prove the commercial viability of the role.

In the end, I decided to take on the role because I trusted Colin. I also thought the riskiness of it made it exciting. The war for talent is every firm's biggest challenge, and I know very few that are good at it. Whoever could crack this would be, well, famous or something. All I had to do then was figure out how.

As you grow, you have to work harder and harder to keep the original sparkle that made you great in the first place. I think all of the senior team here live in mortal fear that we'll start looking like any other two-hundred-person firm. That would be a disaster for us, and fear of failure is very motivating!

In an ideal world, if all of senior management really concentrated on the important things, you wouldn't need my role. I think
you lose it in a fast-growing firm unless you have someone whose
job is to ensure that the style you want is communicated clearly
around the firm.

The problem, of course, is that it's like trying to nail jelly to the
ceiling. You can't plant electrodes on everyone and test how happy
they are when they go home each evening. You have to form a plan
you intuitively believe is right, implement it, and then regularly
check whether it's working.

People always agree that culture is important, but no one is really
sure just *what* culture is. We *call* it culture, because that sounds
sexy, but actually, it's the things that make great people stay. This
bundle of things is different for each person, which is why it can't
be reduced to a staff satisfaction form, or a mission statement for
that matter.

I report to both the creative director and the chief executive to
ensure that the two main areas of the firm are properly represented.
There are no departments that report to me, but I am at the center
of all strategic discussions that have a potential impact on firm culture. I work out a "cultural calendar" each year, which is costed and
must be approved by the board. It helps to make sure that there is a
coherent plan for cultural initiatives and processes.

Each week I e-mail a summary of my activities to the board so
they know on what areas I am concentrating. Additionally, I join
the executive board every other week to discuss issues that have
cultural implications. I am constantly advising the board and other
senior managers to make sure all communications have the right
amount of irony, directness, self-deprecation or whatever seems appropriate.

There is a group of about seven (mostly junior) people selected
from around the firm, called The People's Collective, which agrees
on cultural initiatives, and with my guidance, make it happen. The
group changes every four months to keep the ideas fresh and give
more people the opportunity to contribute. Being in the group is

seen as a great compliment. Its name is deliberately subversive. Cultural initiatives need to feel like they're coming from the people and not the Politburo!

My major initiatives come under two main banners, making this the best working environment in town, and making working for Mortimer Ransford the best possible career move.

Activities coming under the banner of best working environment include renting a boat moored nearby for brainstorming meetings with clients. It may sound minor, or even silly, but it shows that we are constantly looking for ways to take business seriously (have the client meeting) but do it in a way that keeps things fun and fresh (the boat.)

It's a mixture of the basics and the innovative. On the one hand, we have monthly, hour-long firm meetings to explain where the firm is heading, but we also e-mail everyone on Fridays about the week's business and extracurricular news. Every new inductee is assigned a buddy or mentor who makes sure the new recruit meets everyone and understands how everything works.

Like many firms, we have a book that sets out basic information about the firm that is given to each staff member; but we also arrange nights out to film premieres, gigs and shows. We have a charity day where the firm pledges one day per employee to a group of local charities. We also have ad-hoc events like parties and open days.

Activities coming under the banner of "best career move" include:

- ❏ An overhaul of the firm's performance appraisal scheme to reflect balanced scorecard principles.
- ❏ Commitment to a minimum amount of training per year, per person.
- ❏ Recruitment interviews that are treated more than ever as a pitch process, not an exam.
- ❏ Exit interviews with everyone who leaves, in order to be able to fix things that are not right.

❏ A "Down Day" once a year when you can call and say you just don't feel like coming in. This is in addition to your standard holiday allocation. Also, you get an extra week off when you get married.

❏ A satirical internal magazine, the main purpose of which is to make sure no one takes himself or herself too seriously, especially senior people.

❏ A Parents' Day held in mid-summer, so the family members can see firsthand what their loved ones do all day. Colin will dress as a school principal and do spoof reviews, telling to each family how their "little boy or girl" is getting on.

❏ "School trips," a series of days out of the office designed for groups of about twelve people. These include salsa dance workshops, day courses in cordon bleu cookery, and learning how to paint landscapes.

We need to keep doing things that surprise people. We work very hard to counter the fear that growing bigger means growing more *sensible*. But making the place different is only part of the picture. We have a very strong team structure. This gives us great accountability, which drives good client service and financial results.

We were getting excellent feedback about all of our cultural initiatives, including from the people who were choosing to leave. But they were still leaving! So it became clear that we had to take more control of the culture in our teams. The individual small-team leader is probably 80 percent responsible for how the team members feel about the firm. If you don't control this important area, I don't think you can possibly claim to be in control of the firm's culture.

For example, we make it a rule that if you want a career here, you need to have leadership skills. If you don't manage your team well, you may still get a bonus (which is based purely on the financial performance of the team) but your salary will stall, and you'll be denied additional responsibility. Ultimately, you'll lose your job, and we have gone to that extreme.

We have a new set of measures of team leaders that will assess how well they are developing the careers of the people who work for them. We ask, anonymously, for feedback from everyone in the firm with whom each leader comes into contact, including but not restricted to their own team.

We recently had a financial target we wanted to hit, and conventional wisdom would have said to put a "supercharger" on all the bonuses of our key people, to make them work twice as hard to deliver the money. What we chose instead was to allow everyone in the firm the chance to earn rewards (like overseas trips) by going the extra mile, as voted by everyone else in the firm. We had an e-mail address called "the hall of fame" to which people wrote with their nominees. I know that if you're not careful, this can look like a transparent management tool, but so are conventional bonus schemes.

After a period of time, if you do enough of these kinds of activities, your staff stops looking for the negative and starts to realize that this is not a trick. Eventually, if you sustain it, they see that this is a firm that is clearly committed to making it a great place to work. We're not there yet, but I would guess 70 to 80 percent of our people think we're doing this for the right reasons. There will always be a cynical minority who disagree, but I think those attitudes are evaporating fast because they have very few others with whom to substantiate their views.

Eighty percent of my time is spent ensuring middle managers espouse our values. You need to be comfortable with allowing other people to get pats on the back. There is a lot of behind-the-scenes work, like suggesting to a manager that he or she put a Post-it note on a junior person's computer screen for something well done.

What I do *directly* affects 20 percent of our culture, and what I do *indirectly* affects the other 80 percent. Influencing the middle managers, ensuring that they too buy into the principles of the balanced scorecard, means you have a decent chance of making sure you develop your future stars. That, for me, is the most important challenge.

After being trained as an account handler to jump up and down and scream about account wins, all this subtle stuff takes some getting used to. But even the biggest skeptics here are persuaded that the role makes sense for us. Staff turnover was 35 percent before the role was created, and now it's 25 percent. For over a year now we haven't lost anyone we're upset about losing. In the year and a half since this role began, we have doubled our revenue and margin. Word of mouth beyond the firm is working. Every new job opening attracts about twice as many good candidates as a year ago.

We want to make this place uncopyable. From the start we feel we have been writing the book, avoiding the trap of following what other firms have done. We're nowhere near where we want to be, but so far, so good.

What was new here? What have we heard before, and what have we not? Here are one or two of my reflections:

Most obviously, what is innovative here is the very idea of appointing a "culture cop," in part to keep management honest on the ideals it espouses. (I'm not sure this is a good metaphor, but it reminds me of the slave who used to sit behind the Roman Emperors and whisper "Remember, Caesar, you, too, are mortal!")

Like the ombudsmen at Tramster (chapter 2) this company has put in place systems to ensure that management does its job properly, that it practices what it preaches. Most companies worry about systems to ensure that employees do what they should, but how many have methodologies to monitor and hold management accountable? To state the obvious, it is more important to the success of the office that management operates properly; yet few firms have the systems to ensure this.

Another Mortimor Ransford theme, similar to what we have seen elsewhere, is the courage to say "No!" They turn away inappropriate clients, and they have what they call nonnegotiable cultural minimums. As always in these interviews, what is impressive is not the fact that they have standards, but that they have the guts to live up to them.

I know more than a few firms and firm leaders where saying "No!" would be considered a mortal sin. It is inconceivable to them that you could ever be allowed to say "This far, and no further!" to clients, individualists, people who show disrespect to others. One of the scarcest managerial skills may, indeed, be the ability to say "No!"

CHAPTER THIRTEEN

The Effects of Office Size

Is there a difference in average responses for different office sizes?

Surprisingly, none of the *financial* measures had significant differences due to variations in office size. Larger offices were not reliably and predictably more profitable (nor faster-growing) than smaller ones.

However, a number of the questions in the employee survey *did* show statistically significant differences in response by office size, all with strong negative relationships. (The larger the office size, the lower the employee attitudes).

As firms get bigger, a number of factors show a significant *decrease* in the eyes of the staff:

1. Management valuing input.
2. Management listening to people.
3. Management being trusted.
4. Management practicing what they preach.
5. Management being successful in fostering commitment and loyalty.
6. Communication between management and people being very good.
7. People knowing what their office is trying to achieve strategically.
8. Fair and equitable management of the compensation system.
9. Consistently working well as a team.

10. Teamwork.
11. Intolerance for poor performance.
12. Keeping the client informed on business issues.
13. People treating each other with respect.
14. People being encouraged to volunteer new ideas.
15. People having the freedom to make decisions to do their work properly.
16. People expressing their views on issues.
17. High opportunity to move ahead rapidly.
18. People being satisfied with their job.
19. Enthusiasm and morale.

Does this list look familiar? It should. Many of the items on it were identified in previous chapters as key profit drivers.

It's not just minor things that decline with size, but major issues with significant economic impact. What an indictment of larger offices! Anybody want to grow? How about merging?

To look at it another way, five of the nine factors (or question groups) had a statistically significant (negative) relationship with size, as shown in Table 13–1:

Table 13–1: Relationship between Size and Factor Scores

Percent of all differences in Factor Score that can be accounted for by differences in office size

Empowerment	10.8%
Commitment, enthusiasm, and respect	6.6%
Fair compensation	6.1%
Long-term orientation	4.1%
Employee satisfaction	3.4%

The factors that did not have a statistically significant relationship with size were:

Quality and client relationships
Training and development
Coaching
High Standards

(These relationships were also negative, but not big enough to be statistically significant.)

This data suggests why size is *not* correlated with financial performance. While size may well have many marketplace virtues and lend some client-focused competitive advantages, it nevertheless simultaneously creates an organization where it is harder to achieve the employee attitudes that drive financial success. Swings and roundabouts!

CHAPTER FOURTEEN

Bellerephon: A Case Study

Bellerephon is an office of a global public relations firm, based in a city in the U.S. Midwest. Its financial performance index was 73 percent higher than average, driven mostly by stellar margins. Here are the ten items, in descending order, where Bellerephon outperformed the all-office average (by amounts ranging from 19 to 43 percent).

1. We have high-quality training opportunities to improve skills.
2. I am actively helped with my personal development.
3. Enthusiasm and morale around here has never been higher.
4. This place has done a good job of providing the training I've needed to do my job well.
5. Management shows by their actions that employee training is important.
6. Management of our office is successful in fostering commitment and loyalty.
7. Management around here is trusted.
8. There is more opportunity to move ahead rapidly here than is possible at most other places.
9. Communication between the office's management and people at my level is very good.
10. There are real opportunities here for meaningful career and professional advancement.

Here's Alice, Bellerephon's office head, explaining her approach:

Our people know that the more they do together and work as a team, the more the business will grow and the better it will be for everyone. Our office is now becoming a sizable one with momentum. To get here we gave people flexibility, encouragement, ownership and the opportunity to get things done. We trust people. If they have earned the right, they are allowed to exercise their own judgment.

We did a lot of investment hiring, taking the risk of hiring in advance of demand. We put people in new situations and work roles that allowed us to attract some of the best talent in the city. We are very sensitive to people's individual needs. The lesson to the staff is that your work success can earn you wonderful things.

The price of our strategy was taking a chance on people, the cost of hiring in advance of demand. We had to create new positions knowing some would probably not work out. If they didn't, we'd paid salaries with little benefit and had to find new opportunities for those people. But it was essential to get us into niches and submarkets we knew we had to be in.

We estimate it worked out about 60 to 80 percent of the time, which we can live with. The ones that win are usually so strong that the bad bets don't matter.

There is lots of empowerment within our firm to manage your local office your own way. We are hands-on managers here. We are very involved with client work, which is a reflection of our one-on-one coaching approach. It gives us the opportunity to work closely with people as well as on the work itself. It is informal coaching and mentoring.

We coach people continually. We make them understand what is needed, how to grow, and so on. We give them the opportunity to do national things, not just serve local clients. Little of this is done as formal career planning. It is built into the normal weekly interactions we have with everybody.

Our approach is to build our organization and its roles around the people we have and then fill in the gaps around that. We don't believe in introducing set strategies and structures and then insist that they be followed.

We have found that noncash entitlements don't cost much! If you can offer something to employees that gives them more control over their life, it's an effective (and cheaper) way to keep them.

People trust our management because they have continual access to their managers, and get to know them as people, as human beings, not just a person in a role. You must show your vulnerability. Of course, keeping promises when a commitment is made is crucial.

We are strong believers in walk-around management. You can pick up the office buzz, and you can have informal conversations that allow people to know you. It is not a political game here. You live your values. When you get bigger, as we are doing, it is harder to be personal. One way to make it work is to be good at developing lieutenant managers who believe in what you believe in. You sustain the culture because you have developed managers who think like you do.

You have to speak out regularly about your vision and philosophy so people know where you stand. It gives people the confidence that you are sticking with the basics of your promise and then they know how to behave even when you're not there.

A rule we have is that people should feel challenged but not subject to excessive demands. Sometimes, people working the most hours are not as productive as those working fewer hours. Those who put in the most hours often don't engage others in the team. They have an inability to focus during normal allotted hours, so you find them in the office after hours. This is not the right way to work.

Some people just aren't in the right spot or role so we are very willing to give people another chance. We look to see if we can get better performance by placing people in other roles.

We get good marks from our people on training, but that may be because a lot of what we are doing is recently introduced. It's fresh in people's minds. Actually, we still believe that on-the-job learning is the best training. We encourage our people to look back systematically on what they have done.

Enthusiasm is high because we celebrate success and teamwork, and we don't bear down on failures. We have good communication among all the office managers, so there are no cross-group rivalries or politics. At staff meeting we share leadership with junior staff members; they often run the meetings. We share positive client feedback and news about increased business from the client, so we can recognize accomplishments publicly.

We have been creative in allowing work patterns outside the traditional tracks. If we don't make these flexible arrangements, people will go somewhere else, and we don't want that. We believe that you can't be traditional. That is our competitive weapon. We'd like to do more flexible-time arrangements, but the drawback of being a smaller office (of 60 people) is that you can't have more part-time arrangements than the office can handle. We still have to be able to operate effectively and efficiently.

You must invest in your culture as much as your people. Lots of firms will throw huge compensation at someone to get him or her in the door, but then do nothing for or with that person. We think money should be spent on enriching the individual and the team, such as going off-site to learn. Our people know we don't worry about the lost billability that this involves.

We try to run a relaxed atmosphere to let people feel empowered and not under the gun. We want a casual, relaxed, collaborative environment, but also a professional one.

We don't want it to be a silo place. We spend time working to integrate our four groups. You must have one culture. You have to be consistent.

An office takes on the personality of the office manager or leader. Nevertheless, we have learned to back off and let people develop the culture of the office. This is done by letting staff run their own meetings; by having two different middle management groups meet regularly to work on what they think is important for the overall office. They develop the culture.

A lot of the time when people leave us (usually for more money) they come back. Usually, it's because we have a supportive and comfortable environment where they can do good work.

Middle-Management Group

Here are some middle-management people explaining how their office does things:

Why does this office succeed so well? Well, you met Alice, didn't you? Do you really need to know more? She's the key to everything!

She has essential human qualities, like integrity. She walks the hallways and talks not just about work but about you. Sometimes, she just wants to see you, for no reason. She just wants to find out how you are. She remembers everything you ever said to her. If you speak about your personal life she remembers. If you go on vacation, she remembers where you went and makes it her business to come by and ask how it was. She is genuine. Everyone understands that no matter what you go to her with, you will receive an honest answer and it will go no further if you don't want it to.

The manager who was here before her was completely different. He would scream in the hallways. You could not trust him. Everything was discussed behind closed doors.

Alice can be demanding but you respect it because you know her demand is coming from her knowledge of business and is for the common good. She lets you know the reasons behind her thinking. You feel you get whole and considered answers from her—even if you don't agree with what she has to say.

She hires well. She can read people's character and skill level. She knows when she first meets someone if that person will be a good fit and can contribute, or will be disruptive to the office. She's very studied and precise in her talking. She is thoughtful and sincere. She maintains an even emotional keel, and she is always approachable.

We have been either smart or lucky to get challenging business, which helps you learn a lot and be fulfilled. Our staffing at times is tight, so you get responsibility early here. In Alice's early days we hired a lot of new people to get us into new markets, but now, if we lose a senior person, rather than rush to fill the slot quickly, the work is reassigned and everyone pulls together. By taking up the slack ourselves, it allows people to grow.

I left this firm to join a dot-com, for the money. When I got there it was not the opportunity I thought it was. I really never intended to leave here but the money seduced me. I came back because this is a great place to work, and because of the mix of people who you work with on a daily basis. It's also the work we do. I can do things here that you can't do at other firms.

We don't have to worry about politics here. It's an easy place to be. There's an unwritten ethical code of behavior here, which includes no backstabbing, no betraying secrets, no screaming, no door slamming, no shirking or dumping responsibility, and no calling in sick when you're not. An abuse of power or position is a no-no, bullying is considered wrong. None of these are tolerated.

If someone went against our code, a colleague would counsel him or her. We wouldn't wait for management to do it.

In recruiting, we look for a sharing style. The new-hire process is about trying to assess personality and vision. Management doesn't just interview people and say, "Here they are." The whole team does the hiring. If it takes forever to find someone, so be it. We'll wait for the right one.

While looking for a new senior hire, we have been known to use surrogate managers from another office in our firm. We borrow resources, senior or junior, from other parts of our firm.

We have a professionally run training program, but the emphasis here is on lots of mentoring. For example, you might be invited in to monitor a conference call that someone a level above you is having, so that you can see and learn directly how a situation is handled. Interoffice mentoring is available. You can always tap those resources.

There is some mystery around compensation here. There are ranges; but nobody knows the ranges. The office manager and the HR department decide the increases. People generally feel that salary is based on firm profitability. There are two bonus pools: a shared success pool for everyone, based on office results and profitability, and a management incentive pool. The bonus system plays a major role in keeping people happy. It makes us feel we have contributed to the firm and are appreciated for that contribution.

Managers can and do give spot bonuses. Each manager is given a pool at the beginning of the year for this purpose. As a manager, if and when you go to bat for one of your people, you usually get what you propose. If a recommendation is turned down, the reasoning behind the decision is always explained so you understand. This shows respect.

We have a no-hierarchy approach. We are all working managers. The team thing is big; everyone stuffs envelopes. We have the belief that by creating a team, you will work as team and not as a hierarchical group. Individualism is encouraged within a team setting, but you can't exist here as an island.

If someone doesn't show up for team meetings, that would be considered rude and disruptive. If you are making real contributions elsewhere, you might be given a little more slack. But only a little. People who try to make their own rules don't last. When you have an individualist who works on his or her own, it creates tension and everyone feels it. It is not allowed to last for long here.

Team structure and group meetings are meant to be a source of help. They are not a burden. We help each other out. If someone has a personal crisis like a funeral, everyone willingly picks up the slack for that person.

This is an entrepreneurial environment. If you reach out for responsibility, you can create the career you want here. There is a commitment here to the performance review process, which occurs every six months. Feedback mechanisms are very ingrained in the culture. People need to understand where they are and where they need to go, and here they do. There is a real concern here for people as individuals, who they are and what they want. There is a constant dialogue with management about how to get there.

There is no "throwing work on the desk and walking away" by the manager. There is great camaraderie and teamwork, a constant feeling that you are not in this alone. This makes money because people are inspired to work hard because they want to do it. There is a shared pride in working here.

It's okay here for some people to have a job and not a career. At least some people, not a majority. If that is what they want, that's their business. But we don't have many like that.

The theory here is to show concern for the individual, to create a culture of mutual pride. That leads to people wanting a career, not a job. And that leads to commitment and then to the money.

What do you think was worth thinking about here? Here's what I thought about:

"Well, you met Alice, didn't you?"

That phrase has been ringing in my ears since I did this interview. In fact, at one time I was tempted to use it as the book's title. The research for this book beat me over the head with a consistent, insistent message, so I'll do the same to you. It ain't about systems. It ain't about processes. It ain't about tactics. It's about Alice. You want your people to make a lot of money for you? Then set high standards, give them something they can get excited about, and have them managed by someone who is (what did they say?) genuine, cares about them as well as the business (not instead of, as well as), has integrity, and has "a code." It's about character and courage.

CHAPTER FIFTEEN

Age Levels

One of the most fascinating findings of the statistical analysis is this: The views of the younger staff are not only relevant to financial success, they predict it better than do the attitudes of the older employees!

Taking one age group at a time, I looked at the questionnaire scores for each age group and examined how well the views of that age group *alone* could predict the overall office financial performance. (A stepwise regression, the same technique used in chapter 7, was employed.)

The results were dramatic. The views of twenty-year-olds (taken in isolation from the views of others) could explain 54 percent of the variations in office financial performance (independent of geography, line of business or size of office.) The views of thirty-year-olds could explain a similar amount, 57 percent, of the variations in office financial performance. But the views of people forty years and older (age groups were combined here to get a meaningful sample size) could account for only 24 percent of the variations in office performance!

What does this mean? It probably means that knowing whether the senior people think things are going well on various cultural and employee attitude issues does not necessarily tell you much. They probably have a bias for thinking things are going well anyway. Their views do *not* predict profits very well.

Table 15–1: Differences in Response Between Age Groups (Part One)

Age Group	20 to 29	30 to 39	40 to 49	50 to 59
Considering my contribution, I think I am paid fairly compared to others in the office.	−15	−2	+6	+11
Considering the office as a whole, the compensation system is managed equitably and fairly.	−12	−4	+4	+12

However, if you can get the younger employees to believe in your culture, then you've really got something going. It might be major league brainwashing or, more likely, a vibrant, energizing culture with well-understood and effective values. But if the younger people give your office high marks on the issues we have been discussing, there a significantly greater chance of higher financial performance.

The twenty questions with the greatest (statistically significant) differences between age groups are shown below. (All of the survey questions but two displayed a significant difference in responses based on the age of the respondent.)

The numbers shown are the percentage difference from the database average for that question. Thus, in the first row in Table 15–1, people in their twenties agree 15 percent *less* than the average employee that they are paid fairly. People in their fifties agree with that statement 11 percent *more* than the all-age average.

This is probably not too surprising, but the extent of the differences in views is quite striking.

In Table 15–2, we see that most of the factors that define employee satisfaction also show marked differences in age groups.

Table 15–2: Differences in Response Between Age Groups (Part Two)

Age Group	20 to 29	30 to 39	40 to 49	50 to 59
I get a great sense of accomplishment from my work.	–7	–2	+2	+7
The overwhelming majority of the work I'm given is challenging rather than repetitive.	–9	–1	+4	+6
I am highly satisfied with my job.	–8	–3	+2	+9
I am committed to this firm as a career opportunity.	–7	–3	+2	+8
Enthusiasm and morale around here have never been higher.	0	–7	0	+7

If pay and employee satisfaction are markedly lower among younger employees, so too is their perception of management's long-term orientation (particularly if you worry more about thirty-year-olds, rather than twenty-year-olds!) (Table 15–3).

The same pattern exists with regard to training (Table 15–4).

The final three items in the top twenty most significant differences between age groups are a mixed bag, but no less important or interesting for all that (Table 15–5).

One of the interesting things about this listing is the virtual ab-

Table 15–3: Differences in Response Between Age Groups (Part Three)

Age Group	20 to 29	30 to 39	40 to 49	50 to 59
We maintain a balance between short- and long-term goals.	+2	–5	–3	+5
We regularly discuss our progress toward our strategic objectives, not just the financial goals.	+4	–4	–1	+1
I know exactly what my office is trying to achieve strategically.	–5	–5	+1	+8
We invest a significant amount of time in things that will pay off in the future.	+3	–5	–2	+3
The actions of our firm are consistent with ourstrategic objectives and mission statement.	+2	–5	–2	+5

sence of questions about quality and client relationships, and of questions about high standards. On these topics, there is relatively more agreement, it seems, about what is going on among the different age groups. This should be reassuring. However, the differences in perceptions on pay, long-term orientation, and training might be a source of concern!

Table 15–4: Differences in Response Between Age Groups (Part Four)

Age Group	20 to 29	30 to 39	40 to 49	50 to 59
I am actively helped with my personal development.	+4	–4	–4	+4
This place has done a good of providing the training I've needed to do my job well.	+4	–4	–4	+4
Management shows by their actions that employee training is important.	–1	–6	–1	+8
We have high-quality training opportunities to improve skills.	0	–6	–3	+9
Around here you are required, not just encouraged, to learn and develop new skills.	+3	–5	–3	+5

Factor Scores

To explore the age differences a little further, let's look at the average scores given by each age group to our nine factors. (This time, all those over forty were grouped together for statistical validity.)

Three factors show highly significant differences between the age groups (Table 15–6). (Figures in the table use the 6-point agree/disagree scale.)

Table 15–5: Differences in Response Between Age Groups (Part Five)

Age Group	20 to 29	30 to 39	40 to 49	50 to 59
We constantly strive to find innovative solutions to clients' problems.	–2	–2	0	+4
Management around here is trusted.	–2	–4	–2	+8
I often express my views on issues important to me, even when I know others will disagree.	–5	–1	+2	+4

Table 15–6: The Effects of Age on Factor Scores (1)

	Under 30	30 to 39	40 and Over
Fair compensation	3.48	3.83	4.17
Employee satisfaction	3.93	4.21	4.46
Empowerment	4.56	4.70	4.83

Three other factors are also statistically significant, but not in a major way (Table 15–7).

The final three factors do not show statistically significant differences (Table 15–8).

It should now be clearer where the effects of age show up, and where they matter.

Table 15–7: The Effects of Age on Factor Scores (2)

	Under 30	30 to 39	40 and over
Long-term orientation	4.01	3.87	4.06
High standards	4.23	4.25	4.40
Commitment, enthusiasm and respect	3.71	3.74	3.91

Table 15–8: The Effects of Age on Factor Scores (3)

	Under 30	30 to 39	40 and Over
Training and development	3.56	3.55	3.67
Coaching	4.20	4.15	4.24
Quality and client focus	4.70	4.64	4.75

And remember, if you want to know the rules and standards of your culture, ask your twenty- and thirty-year-olds. What they'll tell you has a measurable, statistical, quantitative influence on your financial performance.

CHAPTER SIXTEEN

Arkwright, Sutton: A Case Study

Arkwright, Sutton was another of the highest ranked offices in the study. Its financial performance index was 169 percent higher than average, based on huge growth in the previous two years, while maintaining a margin over three times the norm. Part of a large, multisite firm, this specialized office was physically separate from the firm's other operations. Here are the ten questions, in descending order, on which it most exceeded the results of other offices (from 14 to 22 percent).

1. Enthusiasm and morale around here have never been higher.
2. Management of our office is successful in fostering commitment and loyalty.
3. Communication between the office's management and people at my level is very good.
4. Management around here is trusted.
5. The management of our office always listens to our people.
6. We emphasize teamwork here. Individualistic people aren't tolerated.
7. We have an effective system in place to measure client feedback.
8. We are extremely good at building long-term client relationships.

9. The amount of work I have keeps me challenged, but not overwhelmed.
10. People within our office always treat others with respect.

Here's the office head talking about how these results were accomplished:

The secret of our firm is that we are truly a team effort. Our small size allows us to keep our vitality, be intimate and have everyone very involved with the work at all levels.

This is a different kind of place to work. Everyone participates and work gets attention at all levels. We don't get bogged down in the layers that tend to alienate people. We have no job descriptions, no formal policy and few procedures. We don't tell people how to do things. There are no layers of approval to go through.

As long as the outcome gets achieved, people can do their own thing. Management facilitates, it doesn't dictate. As long as the people come up with new ideas and do good work, I stay away.

A high trust level exists. Politics are at a minimum and will not be tolerated. We have an open door policy at all levels, whether you have a personal or work question. Anything but an open door by anyone in a managerial position would not be tolerated. We have a no-fiefdoms atmosphere. People not only trust management; they also trust each other.

I would fire a person who was Machiavellian and who didn't fit in. I always accepted the maxim that "One should be a little less trouble than one is worth." So if someone doesn't work in our style, they are gone. We don't let anyone fracture our culture for any reason.

To get a high trust environment, we are careful on hiring. We look for smarts, personality and compatibility. They have to be motivated. All our recruitment interviewing here is a collaborative effort. We just know. It's a feeling. When someone says in an interview that they "don't want to be bored," you know that's a clue to a positive hire.

People are rewarded and valued for what they do. Monetary reward is given for the work that people do, not necessarily for the level of their job. If people aren't ready to do something, they are not pushed to do it. People are allowed to grow at their own pace and feel comfortable with what they are assigned or told or asked to do.

To be trusted, you've got to be willing to give up ownership of an idea. The idea will mutate many times before it gets to the client. We stroke each other, and we challenge each other. We trust each other because we support each other.

A client might call and say, "I don't like this." In other places, the boss will call in the staff member and say, "Don't do that again." Here, it is a collaborative effort. We, as management, will get involved. We will get together with the staff and discuss what went wrong, and how we will do it differently next time. We have no tolerance if anyone tries to place blame. Our attitude is "We don't care how it happened, let's just get it fixed."

Managers are trusted to the extent that they back up their people and don't automatically side with the client. But, our people have (and this is a must) an understanding that they will not always win. The difference here is that managers will put themselves on the line with (and for) their people.

We are consistent. We follow through. We don't go back on our word. Managers trust each other. They generally like each other. Lots of discussions take place among us. We support each other and respect each other's work. We have an understanding of each other.

This firm has a very high referral rate for new employees. We don't use headhunters because we don't have to. We have all had experience at other firms, and we try to bring in the best person we know to this one. Trust just comes from working with each other. In smaller firms, people work together a lot to solve client problems. Being small means you're more likely to try to do the right thing for the client. In a small group, everyone is empowered and has ownership of the assignment. As you get bigger, you try to make people feel a sense of belonging to the individual departments.

People think our compensation is fair. We bring people in below market value, with the promise that, if it is successful, the firm will give back. We bring everyone in, at all levels, on a bonus pool and stock reward. We don't have to have the best carpet or new chairs and table. Instead we give money back to employees. People understand that if they work hard there is a reward.

The goal is simple: We want to serve clients as best as we can and make money doing it. Since we don't have a lot of benefits that a big firm can afford, we know that compensation is our biggest key. We use spot bonuses. We reward people right at the time of their achievement. We don't have a system where you know you are going to get a number, say 4 percent, 6 percent or whatever. Such systems are tied to a formal structure, and are rigid and less satisfying to employees.

Rewards aren't just monetary. People are allowed to live lives here so it's not a big deal if someone has to have a day off or have their personal life accommodated. If they have to have a day off for the baby, or banking or whatever, it's okay. There's no backlash.

On evaluations, people understand why they got what they got. People are unhappy when they have no sense of where they are going. What really helps with this is our two-way evaluation system. Both the evaluator and the person being evaluated fill out the same questionnaire. Evaluators must give specifics if they don't score an employee well. But, people here know where they stand on a daily basis and not just at evaluation time. At other places, the negative as well as the positive is often left out. Here feedback on both is given daily.

If someone dropped the ball on evaluations, we would confront it and not tolerate it. We had a woman, a manager, who walked out on a day when the pressure was too much. She just took off, after throwing a verbal fit that everyone witnessed. At the time it happened (and remember she was the manager), everyone else pitched in, stepped up to the plate, did what they had to do to get the job done, and the result was that they exceeded their own expectations.

In the end, I dealt with it and it was a "mutual" decision that this manager would probably be better off elsewhere. After she was gone, it became evident that everyone supported the decision for her not to be there. We hope the soft approach works to get someone to behave as we like, but if it doesn't, we are prepared to be intolerant.

We have honest communication. The reality here is that (to the extreme) our people are fearless in speaking their mind on business or personal issues. No appointments are necessary; there is an open-door policy. People are always comfortable in asking "Why?" about anything going on, and they deserve an honest explanation. No punches are pulled, whether good or bad, and if the answer is honestly "I don't know," then that is what gets said.

I walk the halls and know all the employees. If you are not spending one-third of your time walking the halls, you are not doing your job. Managers should be able to assist others in doing their work and should not have to focus on their own client work.

I regularly give "State of the Union" addresses to the entire office. I let everyone know what is going on. My people know the news before it is public—for example, when we had a merger.

All our people are required to form relationships with client people at the equivalent level. You have got to work side by side with the client or you can't be a partner to that client. It just won't work. Brilliant people who act like prima donnas, who are interested in their work but not interested in clients, are not allowed here. If they can't stand clients, they probably can't stand anyone else!

Socializing with clients is very important if the client wants it. But if the client doesn't, we don't push it or force it. We encourage socializing when it is associated with business, such as going out for lunch, dinner, or drinks.

Other firms try to sell their clients rather than service them. We think lots of other firms have an arrogant attitude. Here presentations are sincere. There is no hard sell. We like the perception to be "She believes in what she says." It is easy to be sincere if you like what you do and you enjoy the process. It is fun to see clients and colleagues succeed, and fun to be part of helping them do it.

I saw a sign someplace that said, "It's about the work, stupid!" My response was, "No, it's about relationships, stupid!" Who wants to work with and for people you don't like? When you really like your co-workers and clients, it makes work a pleasure. If you don't like the people, no amount of compensation can make up for it.

You can't have a relationship with clients with revolving doors of people. If people aren't happy, they aren't going to stay and the result is no consistency with the client.

We have systems to measure client feedback. We utilize an outside phone survey service that surveys all levels of client people from top to bottom. And, the clients like participating! Last year, we got a 100 percent agreement with the statement that the clients would refer others to us. The results of the survey are shared with everyone in the firm.

A crucial element of our success is the belief that relationships, internal and external, are important. People always treat others with respect. Part of it is the skill of listening, and another is the habit of always trying to consider the other person's position.

There is no cross-departmental rivalry. Everyone here is friendly. We have lively debates but no internal walls. Everyone interrupts everyone. There is no standing on ceremony. You don't have to wait until you are promoted to participate. There is give and take in our relationships all of the time.

Disrespect of any kind is not tolerated. People's time and work are respected. There is no suspicion. If someone says they are overloaded and can't get something done, we don't question it. We accept it, and move on.

Work is made as pleasant as possible because that is where you spend most time! We laugh a lot. There are no doors here. We have only two doors in the entire office. It's fun to work together. You must take work seriously but don't take yourself seriously. People think nothing of working over the weekend if the job needs to get done. This is because they like each other. They want to see each other succeed.

It's simple. Respect each other's time. Treat people as adults. Worry about outcomes, not process. Say things like, "We have a deadline. How you get it done is your business. I trust you." If someone says, "Can I have a day off?" we never say yes or no. The response is, "If you think you can go, go ahead."

We don't expect everyone (including ourselves) to be brilliant every day. We let people manage their own time. The workloads here are not less than other places. And don't misunderstand, none of this is about backing off of high financial goals! We're only talking about the best way to achieve those goals.

If there's one thing that stands out, it is that people here are always looking for more empowerment and more responsibility. All of this is about character. Culture is not about systems or tactics; it's a mind-set.

A lot of familiar things, right? At least, familiar in the context of this book, but not necessarily in the real world. But did you spot any new emphases? I think these are worth contemplating:

How about the view that "It's about relationships, stupid! Who wants to work with and for people you don't like?" Absolutely correct, of course, but how many managers and firms make this a real, live operating principle to drive their business? Not many, and they should. It works! You can't motivate an employee you don't like, and it's hard to be excellent in serving a client you don't like. "It's about relationships, stupid!"

And what about this one: "If you are not spending one-third of your time walking the halls, you are not doing your job [as a manager]." Hallelujah, sister! Of course, that's right. The job of a manager is to build an organization that can win business and serve clients profitably. It is not the manager's primary job to try to do these things himself or herself: That's what you do *after* you've completed your primary job of inspiring others to win.

Finally, look at this phrase: "people understand why they got what they got [in compensation]." It turns out, that that's a revolutionary concept!

How fair a compensation system is judged to be is only in small part due to where the dollars flow. More important is whether the compensation-setting process itself is judged to be fair. People want to know that the group doing the judging is diligent and exhaustive in collecting performance information. They also want the *reasons* for decisions that are made to be clearly communicated so that the individual knows what he or she can do better next time to get a better result.

Alas, most firms' version of performance feedback at compensation time is to toss a number over the transom and say "That's what we think of you; figure it out!" (This even happens to partners in many partnerships.) How are they supposed to figure out what to work on to do better? It is surprising how often basic things are done poorly. And it is notable how much our "superstar managers" are achieving their success by doing basic things well.

CHAPTER SEVENTEEN

Additional Comparisons

The Effect of Geography

Of the 74 questions in the survey, 29 had statistically significant differences based on their office location. However, most of the differences are small to modest in scale.

Table 17–1 shows the top 15 scores that differ statistically between the U.S. and non-U.S. offices, organized by size of difference. (All these results are statistically significant results.)

Of the nine factors, coaching, quality and client relationships, and high standards have statistically significant differences depending on office location, as may be seen in Table 17–2.

The fact that there are only a few international differences in employee attitudes provides encouragement that the principles enunciated in this book might have applicability worldwide. People of all nationalities want to be energized and excited at work. While implementation tactics may differ, the things they are energized by (fair compensation, respect, one-on-one management, teamwork and high standards) may be less culture-specific than we sometimes like to pretend.

Lines of Business

Does the performance of offices on such things as culture, management practices and values differ systematically in different businesses?

**Table 17–1: Comparison of U.S. and Non-U.S. Scores
for Top 15 Responses**

Question	Percent that U.S. Offices Scored Compared to Non-U.S. Offices
1. This place has done a good job of providing the training I've needed to do my job well.	+12
2. My immediate manager is an extremely effective coach.	+10
3. My manager is more a coach than a boss.	+10
4. We keep clients informed on issues affecting their business.	+7
5. There are real opportunities here for meaningful career and professional advancement.	+6
6. The quality of work performed for clients by my group is consistently high.	+5
7. We maintain a balance between short- and long-term goals.	+5
8. Management of our office is successful in fostering commitment and loyalty.	+5
9. We have a real commitment to high levels of client service, and tolerate nothing else.	+5
10. I am committed to this firm as a career opportunity.	+5
11. The emphasis in our office is on long-term success, rather than short-term results.	+5

(Continued)

Question	Percent
12. The quality of service delivered to clients by my group is consistently high.	+5
13. The management of our office always listens to our people.	+5
14. We invest a significant amount of time in things that will pay off in the future.	+4
15. Management operates in accordance with the firm's overall philosophy and values: They practice what they preach.	+4

Table 17–2: Comparison of U.S. and Non-U.S. Factor Scores

Question	Percent that U.S. is compared to non-U.S.
Coaching	+6
Training and development	+4
Quality and client relationships	+3
Long-term orientation	+3
Empowerment	+2
Commitment, enthusiasm and respect	+1
Fair compensation	+1
Employee satisfaction	+1
High standards	–4

We should begin by noting that, overall, the financial performance index was *not* correlated with line of business.

Nevertheless, more than 80 percent of the organizational culture responses display significant differences based on the type of business that an office is in. All nine factors differ in a statistically significant manner based on the type of business involved.

As an illustration of the range of differences that exist, Table 17–3 shows the factor scores for (only) three of the lines of business represented in this database. (They have been kept anonymous to protect confidentiality.) The numbers in the table show the *percent difference from the database average* obtained by offices in that category.

What this table reveals is that certain practices do differ significantly from business to business, although these do not translate consistently into different patterns of financial performance.

Stated more strongly, some businesses have historically adopted a more managed approach than others. This is not surprising. For example, law firms (not included in this study) have traditionally not made much use of practice leaders who devote significant time to coaching and managing their groups, whereas this is much more common in, say, consulting and accounting.

Both our statistical and case study analyses of profit drivers are the result of cross-business investigations, and include success stories from a wide range of businesses. This suggests that while historical, cultural differences between businesses are real, there are no inherent barriers in any business to achieving success using the approaches described here.

Leverage

To analyze the effect of an office's leverage structure an index was calculated by taking the percentage of people in the top two compensation levels, and subtracting that from the percentage of people in that office at the bottom two compensation levels.

This index can be positive, indicating a high degree of leverage

Table 17–3: Percent Difference from Database Average on Factor Scores by Line of Business

	Business 1 Percent difference from database average	Business 2 Percent difference from database average	Business 3 Percent difference from database average
High standards	+7	+1	–4
Training and development	+12	–6	–6
Quality and client relationship	+4	–2	–4
Long-term orientation	+6	–3	–8
Coaching	+6	–1	–3
Empowerment	+1	+1	–2
Employee satisfaction	+3	0	–3
Commitment, enthusiasm and respect	+7	0	–7
Fair compensation	+5	–5	–1

(more employees at the lower compensation ranges) or negative, indicating low leverage with more employees at the higher compensation levels.

The correlations were calculated between the leverage index and each of the survey questions, factors, and financial performance index.

Only six of the 74 organizational culture questions appear to be influenced by the leverage of the office.

Surprisingly, as an office became more leveraged, they scored higher on the empowerment questions. This could be due to the fact that where there are many more low-level employees per high-level employee, there is a need for the junior staff to be more self-motivated and empowered. Offices with a low degree of leverage seem to have a slightly tighter feeling of culture and community, and, not surprisingly, they score higher on the assessment of the professionalism of the people.

The degree of leverage plays a relatively insignificant role in the financial performance of individual offices. There are no statistically significant correlations with the financial performance index.

CHAPTER EIGHTEEN

McLeary Advertising: A Case Study

McLeary Advertising is in the recruitment advertising business, with offices throughout the United States. This office achieved both margins and a growth in profit that were double those of the average of the 139 offices in the database. It is a relatively leveraged business with a high ratio of junior to senior employees. Here are the ten survey items, in descending order, where McLeary most outperformed the database average, by amounts ranging from 13 to 22 percent.

1. Enthusiasm and morale around here have never been higher.
2. We regularly discuss the results of client satisfaction feedback.
3. Our management values inputs from all levels.
4. The amount of work I have keeps me challenged, but not overwhelmed.
5. This place has done a good job of providing the training I've needed to do my job well.
6. I am actively encouraged to volunteer new ideas and make suggestions for improvement of our business.
7. The quality of the professionals in our office is as high as can be expected.
8. We consistently work well as a team.
9. We do a good job of delegating work to the appropriate level.

10. I often talk to my superiors about any concerns I might have about my work.

Here is McLeary's office head explaining his approach:

I suspect morale is high around here because we are an extremely friendly place to work, with no hierarchy. We try to ensure that management is approachable. There is an open-door policy, and we have a lot of meetings. We are very structured in some respects, but not as far as approachability goes. We have a variety of forums for the employees to approach management.

People are free to say anything. We might not like what we hear but they are completely at liberty to express themselves. They sometimes grumble because you can't always give them what they want, but they can never say that they are not able to exercise their voice. They may be outwardly unhappy for a while but eventually things usually fall into place.

We want to make this an easy place to work, since we are here for ten hours a day. We are always looking for easier and better ways to do the job or to make the workplace better.

We have a program where we ask people to come up with better ways to do the things they do. We do a lot of procedural things, and employees come up with ideas that will make things quicker and better. Everyone is happy if a new method of doing something is adopted which makes everyone's job or work life better. Usually they just contribute the ideas with no expectation of a reward, although we do have an employee incentive program for such things. They say, "Look I found a better way to do something. It saves time and money and I want to share it with everyone!"

It is important that managers are in the trenches themselves. They see us working alongside them, so they can trust that we understand what they are going through. We are visible, whether we are working on a project with any particular person or not. We are on the floor. We are in other people's offices. Management is walking the halls daily, personally and on a casual basis. It can be a "Hi, how are you?" or it can be an issue.

Spontaneous meetings are encouraged; a lot gets resolved that way. We have designed our new offices to encourage this and be more conducive to an open atmosphere. These spontaneous meetings are central to achieving teamwork. People can come and say I am working on this or that, I need this kind of help. As a manager I am willing to be the intermediary. I am able to go somewhere else in the firm where I know this person can be helped and tell them of the problem and the other person will step up to the plate.

The culture here is not "this is my work, that is your work." We have teamwork because everyone recognizes that sometimes they will need help, so they want to give it too. They know that at any given time they can ask for help through a level above them, and get it. Everyone works together. At times people get so involved in other people's assigned work they they don't pay enough attention to their own, so we have to monitor it!

Albert, our office head, is totally even-keeled, and very even-tempered. At a lot of other places, if something goes wrong and you lose a client, or a big mistake is made with a client, you find yourself getting personally and emotionally upset worrying about how the leader is going to handle it. Here you know how Albert will be, and how he wants everyone else to be. He doesn't run around the office putting the pressure on, or letting everyone know in a frenetic way that "he wants to get this client." Our atmosphere is nice and calm. Albert delivers all news in a non-threatening, non-upsetting way.

If an account is lost, or something very negative occurs, we just try to figure out what went wrong. We try to learn from it. If we lose something, we lose it as a team. There is a formal review of the account to find out what happened, what could have been done to salvage it, if it was a mistake on our part, and thus how to avoid making that mistake again.

We have a very good win/loss record. That is how you grow any business. But if you look at our accounts you will see client longevity and that has a lot to do with what goes on here. When decisions are made on an account they are made together, in a team structure. Clients are very much part of the team.

Overall our attrition is high, at 45 percent, although that's mostly among first- and second-year people. A happy employee doesn't necessarily mean an employee is going to stay. Especially with this new generation there is an attitude of "the grass is greener on the other side of the fence," more than I have ever seen before. There is a lot of searching. A lot of "I don't know what I want to do and I won't know until I find it." The attitude is that if they have been in a job for a while, even if they are doing very well in it, "I am not doing what I should be doing, so I have to leave."

We do have a boomerang effect. A star left and then came back, and it was great for morale. We encourage returnees to talk about their outside experiences. And we have had others who left but we didn't necessarily take them back. The staff usually knows when someone is looking to return and that is good for the culture.

We think this is a happy place because we like to have fun. We all have a good sense of humor and we realize that it is absolutely necessary for our type of work environment. We take the work seriously but we don't take ourselves seriously and we definitely don't take the work environment seriously. Having that atmosphere makes the actual work you are doing more fun because no one is uptight. We laugh at our situations. We rally together.

We give out lots of free food! We have a free candy machine. You know that if you are going to work late, you will be fed. You don't have to worry about that stuff. Some people from other types of firms may come in and say the atmosphere is loud and unstructured. And we are, but it works.

We do have a balance. We aren't the type of firm that throws beach balls and all that new age stuff. We just work hard as team people, like each other, see the work as "ours" and do what we have to do to get it done

Unlike other ad agencies, where someone may be working on the same account five days a week, week after week, we don't have that. We have two-hundred-plus accounts so you are constantly changing what you are doing. There is lots of diversity here so it is tough to get bored.

But if people do get bored, we do something about it. No matter how good someone may be at something, they can get in overload. One person had seven health-care clients at once, and was doing a good job on all. But we looked at her workload and decided that before she burned out we would switch things around so she would have a better variety of work.

It works as a two-way responsibility. We try to look out for the problem, but if we don't see it, it is up to the person to let us know he or she is bored. We then try to fix it. Our employees must take some responsibility to let us know if they are feeling bored.

We do exit interviews, but the funny part is that in the interview people usually say that they liked it here and consider it the best job they ever had, because we have a wonderful group of people. Mostly they leave because other people are doing it and they want to. Or they leave for more money or because they want to be at a dot-com firm, which is where they feel it is "at."

People do come back to visit, to meet their friends or to say hi, and management recognizes that it is a compliment to the firm to see that old people like coming back for whatever reason. We are very social.

We have a lot of referrals for new hires by existing employees, but the trouble with that is that if someone comes to work here because of a friend, that person may leave if the friend decides to. We have one person who does our recruiting and initial screening. She looks for personality and if, in the screening, it appears that the person will not fit into our boisterous atmosphere, they are not considered for the position.

We recognize the need to match culture, and we screen for this. We look for people who laugh and who have a sense of humor. If, on occasion, someone sneaks through that doesn't, he or she will last about sixty days. They usually see themselves that they don't fit in and leave on their own.

It's the same with clients. We have to like the person first before we can work for them. We have to like the client, we have to like the project and they have to like our people before we can work together. We encourage our people to be personal with each other and with the clients they serve. Most client contact is on the phone and it is encouraged and not unusual to hear our people discussing bits of their personal lives and vice versa with the client. This is very helpful to good client relations.

When interviewing new people we also look for a high energy level. If they are to survive our fast-paced industry they will need lots of energy. We have tried hiring people who do not outwardly display a high energy level and they just do not make it.

Occasionally we make a hiring mistake and bring in a high-maintenance person who doesn't operate in all the ways we'd like. We are trying to do a better job of nurturing such people. The reason we don't address this more aggressively is that 45 percent turnover rate. You just figure you can't neglect the others while you try to address the high-maintenance superstar. We need to be mentors to that person, but it is hard. It takes a lot more to make them change their ways because they know they are producing and that in many respects they are very important to the firm because they are money makers.

We are starting to do more and more to get our account managers to be better people managers. We don't have formal training in that area but we are planning to. We know it is something that has to be addressed. The work is fast and the work turnover is fast, so you need to do a lot of constant managing. It is hard to deal with some of the people issues because the time is spent dealing with the work issues to make sure they are accomplished quickly.

We try to do a lot of one-on-one managing and, since we are small, it is easier to address individual problems and issues than to take them up as a group. We try to fit the right people with each manager and the key to doing so is to let the managers hire their own people after the initial screening process has taken place. By doing the actual hiring themselves, they have a stake in that person succeeding so they are more apt to take a deep interest in that person. The managers are not just assigned people.

We find out through clients what their problems are and then we address negatives and positives with the account manager teams. If a client has something positive to say we share it immediately via e-mails, as it comes in. Compliments from clients get transmitted to everyone in the firm, so everyone knows when a client has praised an individual.

On bad feedback, we address it and assess it, either on an individual or team basis. If we find the problem is agencywide, then we do a training session for everyone on the issue to ensure everyone is on the same page.

We have a required twelve-module training program for new-hires. New people get trained in every aspect of the business via these modules. A manager may be assigned to be in charge of a particular module. When anyone gets shaky on an area they can do a review of any of the modules.

We recognize that more formal training has to be done, but we also know there is so much one-on-one mentoring here that it is easy to overlook this as a priority. We have a Manager-in-Training Program so people can grow if they intend to stay. It is for people ready to rise to the next level. They go through training in six different areas, and it is intense and detailed. For this, you have to be selected to participate. It takes six to eight months to complete.

On Thursdays, at five o'clock, dinner is served to everyone. Everyone works late that night due to deadlines for Sunday. You have to be there. A catered buffet is served and everyone looks forward to it. It's not just pizza; we have good upscale dinners.

We have other approaches to keeping morale high. On holiday weekends you can leave a half-day early on Friday. We give paid days off for extra time worked; you get one per quarter. We don't keep track of the extra hours worked to make up that day. We just know that, overall, everyone works overtime and so you get a day.

We have flexibility of hours to a certain extent. People can basically determine their hours.

We have quarterly celebration parties at four o'clock on Fridays, again with good food. We have a bulletin board where we list everything anyone wants to celebrate either for themselves or for someone else. It can be either work-oriented or personal. Birthdays, anniversaries, buying a house or a car, new baby or a big client win, it's anything. This allows personal/professional interaction and is our attempt to make a family atmosphere.

This is where the candidates selected for management training are announced, new employees are welcomed, other promotions are communicated, as is any information anyone wants to share with the firm.

We have a "Meet and Greet" for new employees. Their manager takes new people to lunch. They also are given a formal walk around on the first day.

In the exit interviews what we hear the most about what people liked about this place are friends, camaraderie, energy level and a learning experience. A lot of firms try to steal our people because they do get trained very well here. We see every day as a training experience. Our small size contributes to the high scores for employee energy and enthusiasm. As you grow in size this becomes more difficult. As you grow you need to recognize that you need more managers to be able to do little things.

We assign clients according to a person's experience. We have account assignment lists and these lists are reviewed daily. We work hard to make sure that everyone is satisfied with what they are doing and that above all they feel they can do it. We monitor their comfort with their workload over and over and over, continually. As new clients come in, we don't just assign. We monitor the flow of what they have and of what is anticipated with the new client.

Our people, when given an assignment, never feel that they are left out there to sink or swim, even if the assignment is very new. They know they can speak up immediately if it doesn't feel right.

We make it a legitimate concern to make sure people are not burned out. It's not all noble. I want productive employees and this stuff is all linked with profitability.

Management is involved in workload distribution, studying each client's profitability. We attend weekly team meetings and meet on a regular basis with individuals. We also look at the number of transactions that are occurring per individual on a monthly basis. If it is obvious that someone is consistently struggling and behind we try to address the issue. When we have exhausted all means of addressing their issues, we must do something about it because they just aren't maximizing themselves. But usually, they know it and they leave on their own.

We pay very close attention to our numbers. By doing so, I can look at one particular manager and see that his or her numbers are not what they should be, based on the amount of work being done. I can try to assess what is going wrong before it gets out of hand. The constant monitoring is a key to our success. You can always spend hours and hours on something in pursuit of quality, and it often gets out of hand because you never stop fine-tuning. At some point you have to be able to say, "This is it!"

Everyone wants to see his or her work heralded. But everyone is also made to see how he or she individually impacts the profitability of the agency, so they want to get the product out ASAP. We monitor this.

We have a "red flag" segment to our weekly team meetings when we are addressing profitability. This is the segment of the meeting when people need to report on anything they may have noticed about a client that may affect their serving that client on a timely basis and that will ultimately affect the profitability. This could be as simple as reporting that they are having trouble getting through to a particular person on the phone. We then make sure we work through this. If we have to make a team adjustment we will. Sometimes as a team we go out and reassure the client. But if the client can't work with us, we will walk away from that client rather than compromise our culture.

We are sensitive to clients. If they have been loyal to us we will be loyal to them. We have a client who is presently going through difficult times, and we have adjusted our billing to accommodate them. We practice a no-blame atmosphere. We laugh more than we scream!

We want to make sure that our people communicate with the clients what our firm's core values are. We have a new presentation that managers will give to our people, and the staff will practice it back to us to make sure they'll be giving the client the message we want them to receive. This will ensure that everyone has the same definition of what McLeary is all about, client and employee.

We are sensitive to people's lifestyles. We are compassionate. We take everyone at his or her word. We know that this may be abused at times but for the most part it isn't. We did go through a period when we knew it was being abused, when five or six people all supposedly had doctor appointments on the same day. We addressed it in an officewide forum.

We had toyed with the idea of returning to a more dictatorial "time-keeping" method but decided against it because we knew it was not compatible with our values. The problem just naturally corrected itself once we pointed out that we thought this policy was perhaps being abused. We just can't change our whole way of doing things over a few bad apples.

I really believe that how you treat your people results in how they treat the business back, which results in profitability. They see the value in both the big and little things they are doing, and they will take that extra step for you

The key is close monitoring and observing what goes on. A couple of years ago we recognized that we were having a lot of write-offs, clients saying we had made a mistake so we had to rerun ads at our own cost. To fix this we started having once-a-week proofing meetings where the managers review the work of other managers' teams. This led to team building, and helped profitability as the write-off rate shrank significantly. It also led to camaraderie. We find each other's mistakes and we are so friendly that it is actually fun.

Above all, this is just a nice, friendly place to work, and that is why we achieve our success. We try to be competitive on salaries, but money doesn't keep our people here. We have one competitor that will literally offer any of our people $10,000 to leave. Some, of course, will go, but most don't. It's our culture.

Now we hear from some of the middle-tier people at McLeary:

Our managers are great mentors. Mine encourages me, tells me where I am doing a great job and where I need to learn more. She basically is just a great role model. She is approachable and always there for you. We have an open-door culture here. You can go and speak with anyone at any time, and they listen to you.

We trust management because they can relate to their people and their people feel they can relate to them. When you have an issue, you always know where you stand. They show flexibility, and have a laid-back mentality.

You are informed about and can discuss policies. If you think it should be *xyz* and it is *abc,* they let you know why and this makes it acceptable. Sometimes it is even a little too much because people come to expect to be given a reason for the smallest of items or issues. It depends on the people.

We have good training for new people. When outside trainers come in, they are good professional people who you like to listen to. We have a manager-in-training and professional development training, as well as presentation training. The reason that we appreciate the training so much is that you recognize how much it helps you as an individual and the part it plays or will play in your future. It's considered a reward. They are making an investment in us, especially knowing that there is always the chance we will leave.

Training is on firm time, but clients do come first. If you are supposed to be at a training session and a client problem occurs, you have to deal with the client. We are a deadline industry so in this industry we get overwhelmed, but we have the knowledge that someone will help us. There is teamwork here that most haven't experienced elsewhere. When you yell for help, people come in droves. They set aside their nondeadline driven work and pitch in. They know their time will come, too, when they need help. Everyone understands deadlines.

Also, we have an unwritten policy that in heavy deadline periods, no one leaves until they ask around if anyone needs help. They don't even put their coats on until they have asked, so there is no guilt factor. No one leaves until everyone is finished. We ask. This is enforced. If you don't do this, it will be called to your attention.

Because we are deadline driven and client-service oriented, there is always a mechanism to get the work done if you are out on vacation or out sick. When your team meets they decide who will be your backup when you are out. You meet with the team and give an overview of your work, the status, and so on. A contact sheet about the client and the work is filled out, so the person you leave your account with is prepared.

This takes the pressure off people returning to work. It removes a lot of the backlog. When you are on vacation, you are on vacation. The goal of your team is to promote cohesiveness and support your team first before you support the other team. But we give help to all. Once a quarter each team goes out to dinner and the firm pays for it.

Individuality is encouraged and there is a laid-back atmosphere here in that your time is not necessarily accounted for. They trust us not to take advantage of this. If I am going to see a client, I don't have to prove where I am. Nor will they ever check up to see if you went. You are responsible for your work. People can thrive on little supervision and work well. If you drop the ball, it will become obvious.

There is no baby-sitting atmosphere here. Most people here are focused and are overachievers. There is no micromanaging. Kids who come here straight out of college don't understand that it is not that way everywhere. They don't understand how lucky we are to have the freedom they give us here.

This office is extremely flexible to their employees' outside needs. You don't have to worry about any time-off concerns. For example, one woman became sick and was in the hospital for four weeks. During this entire hospital stay she was paid and it did not come out of her sick time allowance. That is the kind of support that breeds loyalty. This just doesn't happen elsewhere. They also do things like send flowers when you are really sick, or when someone dies.

We have time flexibility when it comes to commuting. They treat it on an individual basis. This is a family-friendly environment. If you have kids, and need to take care of things, they understand. However, the trouble with this is sometimes it is perceived as unfair to those without kids. But we do take care of each other.

We have an Employee Incentive Program, which is a suggestion box with a quarterly award of $100. You suggest process improvements or office improvements, whatever changes you want to see made. Everyone who participates gets a $5 gift certificate to Starbucks. A committee of one manager from each team, a coordinator and an administrative person decide the winner.

Free days off are not recorded, but we get them one day a quarter. You get a personal day and a comp day. It's understood that this is a reward for going beyond the call of duty. They are for account managers who are exempt people and cannot be paid overtime.

We have a new open-door office layout. Also, we now offer a more defined career track and there are more job levels, like junior manager, senior manager and account directors. This makes for higher morale, because you feel like you are working toward something: a goal, a career track.

We all like the quarterly celebration party. Celebrating individuals and their life, both in and out of work, adds to morale. Things to be celebrated are posted on a bulletin board. If you like those you work with, you want to go out with them off-hours and it does lead to team building. If you don't like them, nothing works.

It takes a lot to get fired here. You have to screw up royally for that to happen because they really make an effort to keep it from getting to that level. Everyone is comfortable with those they work for, since they do good recruitment. Rarely does a dingbat get hired. We do have a high turnover rate, so it is hard to gauge morale. In our business, people leave a lot. It's funny now that they are finding out it's not all peaches and roses elsewhere, so people want to come back.

People who leave are sometimes recruited out, often by someone who used to work here. It is flattering to be recruited. Most of those who leave here go to do something different. Some who have left did so because they yearned for a more structured, corporate environment. But that's okay because they probably didn't ultimately fit into our culture anyway.

Was this firm similar to or different from the others we have seen? Many of the themes are similar. Here are some we have not yet highlighted:

"You don't go home until you've asked if anyone needs help." The level of teamwork, of "being in it together" is impressive here. What this firm (and other firms we have examined) has created is a group of people whose commitment is not only to themselves, not only to the firm, and not only to the manager. They are committed to each other: a rare and profitable culture.

I assume you noted in this firm what we heard about before: the boomerang effect. It says something very powerful if a significant number of employees who leave subsequently want to return. Maybe it should be one of the performance measures any firm should use to monitor the health of its culture.

And how many firms can say that their employees view the managers as role models? The answer should be most, but, alas, that's not always true.

CHAPTER NINETEEN

Julie's Perspective

During her thirty-year career, Julie MacDonald O'Leary, my business manager, has had experience being an "employee" in a range of settings (law, accounting, politics, radio, travel, health care and academia). She assisted me with all the case study interviews in this book, so I asked her to list the special points of interest that stuck out in her mind. Here, in no particular order, are what she believes are the most important lessons:

1. Don't be afraid to live your values.
2. Don't be afraid to bet on the long term even if it means sacrifice to the short term.
3. Have fun. At most of these places the atmosphere is one that makes people look forward to coming to work because it is fun to be there. It's not about the work—it's about the environment. Having people want to be at work is a key to success.
4. Monitor attendance at Christmas parties, summer outings or other group events. It's a better barometer for employee morale than any survey. Good feelings about the workplace (and about management) are the result of people believing that management has a good feeling about them. Activities such as parties, manicures, whatever, enhance this. Having happy employees results in motivation and retention.

5. Know who and what each person is about, personally and professionally. Be sensitive to your people's personal lives and issues and treat them with the same respect and allowances that you would want for yourself.

6. When hiring, look for shared value systems and compatibility. (Ask most people what they miss most about a former workplace, be it a negative or positive experience for them, and they'll say "the people.")

7. No dictating; no disrespect; no hierarchy; no politics. Have respect for everyone and for the role they play. Have an atmosphere where people can speak up without any fear and backlash.

8. Follow through and deliver on your promises. Broken promises are remembered more than kept ones. Do what you say you are going to do. If ever you can't, make sure it is understood why you can't deliver.

9. Create intimacy. No matter what your size, try to maintain an environment that enables you to function as smaller size places do to create a tightly knit group.

10. Treat people like grown-ups. Trying to pull rank or use power inappropriately with your people only breeds disrespect for you. That there is a hierarchy is a given. It's how it is executed that counts.

11. If somebody is struggling with something, realize that maybe this isn't the job for that person, and don't be afraid to reassign him or her, without penalty. (This is *big!*)

12. Allow freedom of time, autonomy in time management. Knowing one has input into the "order of the day" results in better work.

13. Use boomerang and alumni situations to your advantage. Realize that former employees, who continue to take pride in having worked for you and who left with a good feeling about the place, make a powerful statement about

management. When people wish to return to your employ, it makes even a stronger statement.

14. Remember that one sign of a good work environment is that people don't leave for more money even when they know they can. (After reading the case studies, ask yourself why!)

15. Make sure you like your clients and what they are doing so you can believe in your work. Don't be afraid to drop a client.

16. Listen to people. Being listened to and being kept informed breed respect and skills.

17. Maintain open doors and accessibility. You're not allowed not to be approachable.

18. Be a magnet person; be someone who makes people want to stay. Be a mentor and a role model. Set the example.

19. Use a one-on-one approach. That's what makes an impact and causes change.

20. Use all levels of people to establish and maintain your culture.

21. *Back* your people, and don't make last-minute changes. But if you must, ensure that your people understand the change, buy into it and are willing to do it.

22. Write three things that keep you awake at night about the client. Then have your people write three things that keep them awake at night about you, the workplace, etc. (Be brave!)

23. Build around the people you have. Exercise their strengths in growing your business.

24. Focus on personal development training vs. technical training. On-the-job training is the best. Don't cancel training for anything.

25. Use the "Doctor Is In" brainstorming exercise. Have others available to help a team that's stuck.

26. Monitor appropriately at work. Don't baby-sit, allow autonomy with guidance (when necessary). Reward and reinforce a person's individual pride in their work.
27. Don't push people too far. Sometimes when profitability is too high, it means they are working too hard.
28. Don't let talent outweigh personality.
29. Don't allow individual interests (especially your own as manager) to be placed ahead of the overall interest of everyone.
30. Have smaller client rosters but with deeper client roots.
31. Create interdepartmental projects. Cross-boundary stuff makes for teamwork.

CHAPTER TWENTY

Lessons: The Manager

In this chapter, we shall summarize and explore four groups of comments that relate to the individual manager: (1) what managers must be; (2) What managers must believe; (3) What managers must do; (4) Other things expected of management.

If you highlighted phrases with a yellow marker as you read the case studies in this book, you can probably assemble your own lists like those that follow. These lists sum up the philosophy, the goals and the practices of the heads of the most successful offices in this study. You can use them as a quiz. How many of these things do you do? How many do you do well?

What An Effective Manager Must Be

The people in our successful offices were both articulate and precise about what the individual manager needed to be. Notice, not "do," but "be." Consider circulating this list, and asking those around you whether you *are* these things.

❏ A good communicator
❏ A good listener
❏ A role model
❏ A magnet for talent (the reason people want to stay)
❏ Accessible all the time
❏ Apolitical

❑ Articulate about what you stand for
❑ Comfortable with allowing other people to get credit
❑ Disciplined about standards, although open to reasons why
   they may not be met
❑ Enthusiastic
❑ Even-keeled and even-tempered
❑ Genuine
❑ Good at reading people's character and skill level
❑ Honorable
❑ Noble
❑ Sensitive to personal issues
❑ Smart, but human
❑ Someone of high integrity
❑ Studied and precise in your conversations
❑ Thoughtful
❑ Sincere
❑ Transparent, not opaque
❑ Unquestionably honest

This list poses an interesting challenge. What can you do about the fact that what you *are* as a person probably accounts for a significant portion of your business's success? It seems to suggest that, if you want the people in your business to respond differently (i.e., raise their performance), the place to start is to look into your own heart and ask what kind of person you are, and how you come across to others!

Try this. Start by checking all the statements above. Then convene one-on-ones, or small group meetings, with your peers or with those you manage directly, and have candid discussions about the contradictions, if any, between how you see yourself and how others see you. Find out if you fall short, and if so, precisely how. (You can do this with a survey if you think such a meeting might be too awkward.)

What Managers Must Believe

More than the other three categories in this summary, this section contains the real messages of the superstar companies. As was said repeatedly, success comes not from specific tactics but from the mind-set, worldview or belief system that lies behind them.

This is not necessarily a pleasant message. Tactics you can adopt, change, put on and take off. But a philosophy? You either believe this stuff or you don't. Or, more importantly, either your people believe that you believe this stuff, or they don't. That's the test!

Try it as a real test. Circulate this list (or your modification of it), and ask your people whether or not they think you act in a way that reflects these beliefs. One way or the other, you'll make some interesting discoveries!

Managers of the successful firms we have looked at believe that:

- ❏ First, you build your people and the rest will come.
- ❏ You must care about things happening in your people's lives.
- ❏ You must have a real concern for people as individuals, who they are and what they want.
- ❏ *Chasing* money is not what *makes* you money.
- ❏ Development of people precedes and has a greater priority than profits.
- ❏ Eighty percent of everything is choosing the right person.
- ❏ Ethics have to be the bedrock that you start from.
- ❏ First give respect and you will get it.
- ❏ Good people management leads to longevity, which leads to client trust, which leads to more business.
- ❏ You must have a sense of humor about yourself and about work.
- ❏ If you have the right client base, the right people with the right attitudes, and the right systems, the money will follow.
- ❏ You must ensure that the workplace is a comfortable, friendly place to be.

❑ Success is about character, respect, integrity, trust, honesty, empowerment, confidence, loyalty and keeping promises.

❑ It is easier (nowadays) to replace clients than good employees.

❑ It takes emotional courage to be a good and improving manager.

❑ It's not just about the work; it's about relationships, stupid!

❑ It's important how people treat each other; monitor it and manage it.

❑ It's more fun to work in groups.

❑ You must keep a good balance between focusing on people, clients and the finances.

❑ You must live up to your values every day.

❑ You must ensure everyone has fun doing what they do.

❑ People must not only trust management; they must also trust each other.

❑ People who leave will come back if you have a supportive and comfortable environment where they can do good work.

❑ Success is due to small size, empowerment, profitable projects, and interest in the individual.

❑ The nicer you can make it at work for people, the better it is for your profits.

❑ The real issue is the willingness to bet on the long term, and not get stampeded by short-term pressures.

❑ It is the combination of fun and discipline that gets the job done.

❑ To manage well, one's interest in people needs to be above average.

❑ You can sustain a culture if and only if you have developed managers who share your values.

❑ You can't have good client relationships with revolving doors of people.

❑ You have to do great work and treat people well. It's not one or the other.

❏ Your agenda as a manager is to create a great place to work, rather than work at making your own meteor rise.

Do your people believe that you believe these things? Ask them!

What Managers Must Do

In addition to what you must *be* and *believe*, the case studies presented here offer some very concrete advice about what individual managers must *do*. Do your people think you do these things?

❏ Act as if not trying is the only sin.
❏ Act as if you wanted everyone to succeed.
❏ Like your people, and be nice to them.
❏ Actively help people with their personal development.
❏ Allow people to exercise their own judgment.
❏ Allow people to learn from their mistakes without retribution.
❏ Allow people to speak out no matter what their role is.
❏ Allow your people to try different skills and experience different things.
❏ Always do what you say you are going to do.
❏ Always put focus on the other person.
❏ Respect the other person's time.
❏ Make sure feedback mechanisms are ingrained in the culture.
❏ Believe in, and keep the faith with, what you are doing.
❏ Watch the pulse of things, so there is no need to come in at the last minute and make huge changes causing disruption.
❏ Do what is right, long term, for clients and for your employees.
❏ Do your own photocopying, when necessary. Wash your own cup.

❑ Don't be "separate and distinct" from your people.

❑ Don't expect your employees to do anything you wouldn't do yourself.

❑ Don't hesitate to jump in and help.

❑ Never talk down to anyone.

❑ Facilitate, don't dictate.

❑ Put yourself in your employees' shoes and know what they are going through.

❑ Give credit where credit is due.

❑ Give whole and considered answers.

❑ Have an open-door policy at all levels for personal or work questions.

❑ Lead by example; be what you want others to be.

❑ Manage people in the way that works for each individual, not just the way you like to manage. You don't have to be a chameleon, just adaptable.

❑ Manage with an upbeat personal style, but keep a level emotional keel.

❑ Deliver bad news in a non-threatening, non-upsetting way.

❑ Never become detached.

❑ Remember what people tell you.

❑ Understand what drives individual people.

❑ Respect confidences.

❑ Respect the need for people to have their own space.

❑ Show enthusiasm and drive; they are infectious and addictive.

❑ Take work seriously, but don't take yourself seriously.

❑ Treat all roles as equally important.

❑ Treat everyone's opinion as vital.

❑ Treat people as adults.

❑ Treat people who leave respectfully and with appreciation for what they have done for your firm.

❑ Work the halls and know all the employees. Spend at least one-third of your day doing this.

❏ Show levity and a good sense of humor.
❏ Speak regularly about your vision and philosophy so people know where you stand.
❏ Let people know you as a human being, not just as their manager.
❏ Act on the principle that all effective management is one-on-one.
❏ Show your vulnerability.

Again, do your people think you do these things? Routinely?

Other Things Expected of Management

We're not done yet. There's still more expected of the individual manager. Here's the remaining advice.

❏ Ask people regularly whether they feel they have good role models in the office.
❏ Be demanding but make sure your demands are driven by the common good, not your personal interests.
❏ Be willing to take money from short-term profits to fund employee satisfaction.
❏ Build your organization and its roles around the people you have and then fill in the gaps around that.
❏ Concentrate on the positive; don't emphasize the negative.
❏ Conduct all exit interviews personally.
❏ Create a "casual, relaxed, collaborative" environment, but also a professional one.
❏ Develop bench depth so you have greater slack in the business, and more freedom to avoid short-term thinking.
❏ Don't allow senior people to "throw work on the desk and walk away."
❏ Don't have hidden agendas.
❏ Don't make last minutes changes in your people's work before it goes to the client.

❏ Don't make what you know is a wrong decision just to hit a short-term financial goal.

❏ Don't put good, cool people into a dull situation.

❏ Earn trust by providing continual access to managers.

❏ Be an intermediary for your people to get cooperation for them from elsewhere in the organization.

❏ Ensure that managers are in the trenches themselves.

❏ Establish an ombudsman or a liaison, as a lifeline to what is going on.

❏ Get people to trust you by really caring about them and their development.

❏ Give no "brownie points" for *exceeding* workload and revenue targets if this risks "burnout."

❏ Make sure people view you as the someone they would like to have as a neighbor.

❏ Make sure upper management is not concerned with demonstrating their status.

❏ Make sure your people know the firm will take care of them.

❏ Back up your people and not (automatically) the client.

❏ Spend most executive committee time on HR issues.

❏ Offer high recognition, psychic rewards and monetary rewards.

❏ Send a strong signal to your staff that the guys at the top are not afraid to make the difficult decisions.

❏ Be the reason people want to stay.

❏ Show sensitivity to what staff are going through.

❏ Support and back up your staff and their decisions.

❏ Walk the halls, continuously talking not just about work but about "them."

❏ When you get angry (which should be rare), ensure people know why.

CHAPTER TWENTY-ONE

Lessons: Creating the Success Culture

Intolerance

A notable fact about both our survey and the case studies is the number of times strong, non-compromising words like "require," "insist," "demand," "nonnegotiable" and "enforce" appear. The following list might look obvious, because no one can be *for* the things it lists.

The message is not simply that you should be *against* these things. You must be completely, absolutely, unquestionably intolerant of them. And further, you must successfully convince everyone in your office that you are intolerant of them. Why not ask them?

You must not tolerate:

❑ Abuse of power or position
❑ Any disrespect shown by anyone to anyone else
❑ Anyone who is abusive
❑ Backstabbing
❑ Being late to meetings
❑ Betraying secrets
❑ Bullying
❑ People calling in sick when they're not
❑ Cross-departmental rivalry
❑ Cruising
❑ Dealing in blame

❑ Derogatory statements
❑ Disrespect of any kind
❑ Freak clients, where there is the potential of failure from a relationship standpoint
❑ Clients that aren't exciting
❑ Clients who abuse your people
❑ Clients who don't treat your people well
❑ Gossiping, whining, complaining
❑ Hiding from accountability
❑ Lack of teamwork
❑ Management through intimidation
❑ Managers who are not good coaches
❑ Noncompliance with standards
❑ Not treating people with respect
❑ People who are "snappish" with anyone else. If they are, insist they apologize
❑ People who try to make their own rules
❑ Screaming
❑ People who don't hold up their end of the deal
❑ Shirking or dumping responsibility
❑ Those who are political

On reading this list, a good friend asked me several questions:

1. What forms *should* intolerance take?
2. How should one be intolerant?
3. What are the right phrases for socially acceptable intolerance?
4. Should you ever chew out someone publicly?
5. What would constitute a firing matter?

I'll have more to say about how to be intolerant in chapter 25 (The Courage to Manage). For now, perhaps the best illustration of brilliantly executed intolerance is given in *Goldman Sachs: The*

Culture of Success, by Lisa Endlich. She describes a young banker, eager to shine, who kept her supervisor posted on every trade and deal she did with notes saying, in effect, "I did this!"

After a while, her supervisor happened to pass her in the hallway and casually said, in a low, soft-spoken voice, "At Goldman we say We, not I," and moved on. The young banker got the message.

Intolerance is about responding quickly to any and every instance of noncompliance with standards. The course of wisdom is start out with a gentle reminder of the standards. If this fails to work, then a more intense private conversation is held. ("You seem to have an issue with acting in accordance with our standards. How can I help?") While one should never chew someone out publicly, the insistent coaching must escalate in intensity and urgency until the individual either returns to compliance with the standard, or is asked to leave. The ultimate sanction must usually be imposed within two years if the standard is to be seen as credible.

What You Must Require

As hard as it is for managers to live up to the personal standards already outlined, there is, in fact, a harder task for the manager. He or she must ensure that *everyone else* behaves appropriately. This takes a lot of courage. It means counseling, cajoling, confronting, monitoring, critiquing, energizing and convincing other people in the organization, especially other senior people.

One way or another, managers in our shining success offices make sure the following standards are maintained.

- ❏ People's attitude is: "We don't care how it happened, let's just get it fixed."
- ❏ All employees form relationships with client people at the equivalent level.
- ❏ Continual career development for everyone.
- ❏ Everyone practices diplomacy; courtesy; professionalism; without superficiality.

❏ Everyone must be a team player.

❏ Everyone must be approachable.

❏ Everyone must be self-motivated.

❏ Everyone must develop leadership skills.

❏ Everyone must learn new skills continuously.

❏ Everyone must respect their colleagues and be cordial.

❏ Everyone's voice must be appreciated and heard.

❏ If a performance review doesn't get done on time, the manager's "bonus" should be reduced significantly.

❏ If people don't manage their teams well, put a hold on their salary, deny them additional responsibility, and if that doesn't work, fire them.

❏ Insist everyone work together for the overall success of the firm, not just themselves or their group.

❏ Make sure everyone knows they must be reliable. If you take something on, then you must deliver.

❏ Management should do what they say they are going to do.

❏ Management should be made up of "high integrity" people.

❏ Everyone must show respect for other people, inside and outside.

❏ Talent is no excuse for bad behavior.

❏ Try the soft approach to get someone to work to your standards, but if it doesn't, be prepared to be intolerant.

To achieve all this, you may need to alter the beliefs of those within your organization, or instill new beliefs. How can you get someone, for example, to truly believe that talent is no excuse for bad behavior? There are several answers, and they do *not* include skills-based training and lectures, although it may be necessary to convene a meeting to communicate and discuss your own determination to enforce your cultural values. The ultimate answers, however, are one-on-one counseling, coaching and being a shining role model.

Creating a Community

What was notable about all of our case study offices was that there was a real sense of "being in this together." These were not random collections of people who happened to work in the same firm. They were true communities. Equally clear was the fact that this was not by chance. The managers involved set out to create such a sense of community.

Notice that this is not just about teamwork, or collaborating on assignments when necessary. It goes far beyond that in the most profitable places. We're talking about true communities where people feel a mutual sense of responsibility and obligation to support each other, and each accepts his or her fair share of the responsibility for joint challenges the enterprise faces. It's rare, and it's powerful stuff to behold!

Here, according to the best, is how to achieve this kind of community.

- ❏ As you get bigger, have people you have developed (and who share your values) manage for you.
- ❏ As you get bigger, work at building loyalty to a person's individual department.
- ❏ At staff meetings talk about the numbers. Give them the plan.
- ❏ Award weekly prizes for making the week's best nonfinancial contribution to the firm.
- ❏ Create "task forces" for all changes in the firm.
- ❏ Create a culture of mutual pride in each other's accomplishments.
- ❏ Have a formal system to arrange backups when a person is scheduled to be out.
- ❏ Make sure people believe management is not *only* out to make a lot of money for themselves.
- ❏ Enforce the rule that people don't leave until they ask around if anyone needs help.

❑ Discuss all financials (except salaries) with everyone.

❑ Earn trust by supporting each other.

❑ Encourage everyone to know things about each other's personal lives.

❑ Have a bulletin board where you post everything anyone wants to celebrate either for themselves or for someone else. This is where the candidates selected for management training are announced, new employees are welcomed, and promotions are communicated, as well as any other information anyone wants to share.

❑ Encourage group decisions.

❑ Ensure employees understand and care about the success of the business.

❑ Ensure everyone cares as much about everyone else's group.

❑ Ensure everyone feels pride and ownership for the firm and for what they do.

❑ Ensure everyone knows why a decision is made.

❑ Every Friday afternoon, get everybody together and review the week.

❑ Everyone eats together in the lunchroom at a fixed time.

❑ Expect everyone to know how their co-workers' lives are going and what they are doing, both personally and professionally.

❑ Face successes and failures as a group, as a firm.

❑ Give employees a sense of pride in shooting high.

❑ Give everyone a lot of exposure to the leaders so they know who they are.

❑ Give regular "State of the Union" addresses to the entire firm.

❑ Have a system of staff sharing, where the managers of different groups take collective and joint responsibility for the whole office.

❑ Have a very active program of cross-functional information sharing, using briefs, e-mails, lunches, whatever.

❏ Have good communication among all the office managers, so there are no cross-group rivalries or politics.

❏ Have middle-level groups meet regularly and work on what they think is important for the overall office.

❏ Have monthly group meetings and practice meetings to address business issues and to explain where the firm is heading. Give everyone a chance to laugh at themselves.

❏ Hold informal tableside chats randomly with people from all levels.

❏ Invite the staff's family members to the office to see first-hand what their loved ones do all day.

❏ Involve everyone in everything you can.

❏ Judge mid-level team leaders on creating a collaborative culture for their team.

❏ Keep everyone informed and in the loop.

❏ Keep groups small, since it is easier for a manager to make an impact on people; it allows everyone to be intimate and very involved with work at all levels.

❏ Let junior staff people run your meetings.

❏ Let people know the reasons behind your thinking.

❏ Make a lot of use of cross-boundary teams.

❏ Practice financial transparency with the staff.

❏ Send e-mails to tell everyone on Fridays about the week's business and extracurricular news.

❏ Set standards and then live those standards.

❏ Share accountability all the way to the top.

❏ Share all successes and failures with everyone.

❏ Show a clear commitment to development of staff.

❏ Spend time working to integrate your different groups.

❏ Take the time to interact socially, even if just in the hallway.

❏ People should trust you to look out for them, even at the sacrifice of your immediate interests.

❏ Encourage great camaraderie and teamwork, a constant feeling that you are not in this alone.

❏ Create fun and enjoyment at work.
❏ View goals as collective; no egos allowed.

Remember, these are not just arbitrary rules of good people management. These are the practices of the most profitable offices in this global database!

CHAPTER TWENTY-TWO

Lessons: Developing People

Our survey and case studies made it obvious that the best managers paid careful attention to developing their people. The staff in our case studies made repeated reference to the importance of this in creating their loyalty and dedication. They made a number of important recommendations:

❏ Hold senior people accountable for how well they are developing the careers of those who work for them.

❏ Be rigorous about "on time" performance reviews.

❏ Encourage others to take over your projects (i.e., delegate).

❏ Encourage people at all levels to do more and more as time goes on.

❏ Encourage your employees to be involved at *all* levels of decision making.

❏ Have a variety of forums for the employees to approach management.

❏ Encourage your people to be fearless in speaking their mind on business or personal issues.

❏ Ensure lots of risk taking. Always push the envelope.

❏ Ensure people realize that if they reach out for responsibility, they can create the environment they want. Give people flexibility, encouragement, ownership and the opportunity to get things done.

❑ Give people the ability to do their own thing, and if you don't agree, give them the right to discuss.

❑ Have a commitment to the performance review process. Establish a two-way review system in which both the evaluator and the person being evaluated fill out the same questionnaire.

❑ Help people understand what is needed and how to grow. Don't assume they know.

❑ Hold people accountable for fulfilling their responsibilities. Allow nothing to fester.

❑ Invite junior people in to monitor a conference call that someone a level above is having, so that they can see and learn directly how a situation is handled.

❑ Let people define their own work and build their own roles.

❑ Make public commitments about initiatives and actions; keep people informed in real time.

❑ Move people from team to team.

❑ Once a year have a formal sit-down with each person and talk about what he or she likes to do and what he or she wants to work on. Work hard to find out what people like and try to accommodate them.

❑ Ensure people know where they stand on a daily basis and not just at evaluation time.

❑ Be very willing to give people another chance. (Some people who look as if they are not succeeding just aren't in the right spot or role.)

❑ Actively work at helping people "dream," and make it fun.

❑ Understand that employees are looking for help from managers in growing their career.

❑ Use your own client work as a chance for one-on-one coaching.

❑ Ensure that all managers are "boosters," people who will say, "You can do it, you can do it!"

Creating an Energizing Workplace

Another hallmark of our successful offices was their ability to create the energy and enthusiasm for work that clearly accounted for their financial success. Here are their suggestions for creating an energetic (and energizing) workplace:

❑ Allow employees more control over their lives.

❑ Measure (and react to) employee attitudes and concerns on a regular basis.

❑ Allow employees to explain where they want to be, and try to accommodate them.

❑ Ask each person, "Where do you want to go next? What are the resources that you need?"

❑ Encourage everyone to grow with the job.

❑ Encourage those who have left and returned to talk about their outside experiences.

❑ Ensure *everyone* is going to do 100 percent. Don't tolerate less.

❑ Ensure people have a sense of where they are going.

❑ Allow middle-level managers the freedom to do what they have to do in order to improve morale.

❑ Stroke each other, and challenge each other.

❑ Be willing to give up ownership of an idea.

❑ Challenge conventional wisdom in every facet of the business.

❑ Be creative in allowing work patterns outside the traditional tracks.

❑ Celebrate success and teamwork, and don't bear down on failures.

❑ Watch closely for people who may be getting bored, and reassign them.

❑ Avoid telling people *how* to do things, unless absolutely necessary. As long as the "outcome" gets done, allow people as much freedom as possible to do it their way.

❏ Don't focus on job descriptions and formal policy and procedures.

❏ Eliminate nonproductive things like too many meetings.

❏ Ensure everyone knows that the firm will support them.

❏ Have disrespect for titles and hierarchy.

❏ Have it understood that no matter what they come to you with, your people will receive an honest answer and it will go no further if they don't want it to.

❏ Middle managers who go to bat for one of their people should usually get what they propose.

❏ If someone goes on vacation, remember where he or she went and make it your business to come by and inquire about it.

❏ If someone makes an error, don't jump on him or her.

❏ Adopt the attitude: "You will not get penalized for doing something, only for doing nothing."

❏ If you lose a person, rather than rush to fill the slot quickly, reassign work to give more responsibility to those who did not have it.

❏ Let your people be the best judge of their own priorities.

❏ Let your people manage their own time; try new things; have a long rope; do their own thinking; run their business.

❏ Make people superworkers by helping them do the kind of work they want to do.

❏ Make sure it is an intense work experience at your firm.

❏ Motivate by enthusiasm and energy, not by telling people "you need to be energized."

❏ No spoon-feeding. Expect people to step up to the plate and fix their problems without waiting for someone to tell them to do it.

❏ Challenge people but do not subject them to excessive demands.

❏ Send handwritten notes to everyone on their anniversary with the firm.

❏ Give people honest explanations of everything that is happening. (They are always curious about anything going on.)
❏ Loosen up. Don't stay in your role all the time.
❏ Give people ongoing feedback along with more in-depth guidance of "how to" develop.
❏ Allow people to grow at their own pace and feel comfortable with what they are assigned/told/asked to do.
❏ Overhaul your firm's performance appraisal scheme to reflect balanced scorecard principles.
❏ Try to do personal things for your people.
❏ Regularly ask your employees which one person is the magnet for them to stay.
❏ Promote managers from within.
❏ Promote people by having their supervisor give a two-minute personal testimony to the group about the person.
❏ Make sure people know where they stand in performance.
❏ Provide flexibility about what people want to work on and what their personal issues are.
❏ Provide opportunities to move ahead rapidly.
❏ Push to be on a leading edge, always trying to do something different and better.
❏ Put people in new situations and work roles.
❏ Put people together from different disciplines.
❏ Recognize achievement immediately.
❏ Recognize that work life and home life need to balance.
❏ Regularly interview people at all levels in the organization.
❏ Resign clients who do not show respectful treatment.
❏ Showcase good work. Show people the difference between good work and "good enough" work.
❏ Sometimes, drop by just to see people. No reason. Just to find out how they are.
❏ Speak freely to allow people to relax and feel comfortable to do their jobs.
❏ Speak regularly with everyone individually about his or her pay and performance.

❏ Take a moment and say "we need a time out." People need to have some fun.
❏ Emphasize the positives of each person.
❏ Prove that management cares, that the staff are people and not just bodies to be burned out.
❏ Run a relaxed atmosphere (and be relaxed yourself) to let people feel empowered and not under the gun.
❏ Walk away from a client if it is not fun, creative and exciting.
❏ When a subordinate's recommendation or request is turned down, always explain why.
❏ Work hard to give everyone a fair chance.

Appreciation and Other Nonfinancial Rewards

I am sure you noticed that the people who worked in our success offices felt that their efforts were appreciated. Managers can create that feeling in a number of ways:

❏ Allow "down days," which means once a year you can call and say you just don't feel like coming in.
❏ Be willing to give time off if it is needed for personal reasons or for a job well done.
❏ Consistently thank people for a job well done and give them a pat on the back.
❏ Express appreciation on an informal, continuous basis.
❏ Give "Thank you's" every day.
❏ Give people an extra week off when they get married.
❏ Have a sabbatical leave program for everyone, when people can do whatever they want.
❏ If someone comes up with a good idea that gets used, give him or her a gift certificate.
❏ Reward people with more diversified work by giving them more stimulating work and with different opportunities.
❏ Show appreciation for even small accomplishments, as soon as they happen.

❑ If a client has positive things to say, share them immediately via e-mails.

❑ Ensure that compliments from clients get transmitted to everyone in the firm, so everyone knows when a client has praised an individual.

❑ Show appreciation, not just with money but in small ways like sharing between teams and e-mail "thank you's."

❑ Worry about outcomes, not process.

Creating Fun

Wasn't it interesting how many of the firms we looked at engaged in "tacky" events like parties, days out and other similar activities? I can imagine some of my more conservative clients among the professions thinking that these things are beyond the pale. But is it so strange to think that the workplace can be fun? Is fun really incompatible with hard work, or does it facilitate it? In any event, here's what our superstars did:

❑ Arrange a series of group days out of the office.

❑ Constantly merchandise the firm to their people.

❑ Create "Moments of Fun."

❑ Eat lunch together every day as a group.

❑ Hold a Spring Break party.

❑ Have a charity day where the firm pledges one day of volunteer work per employee to a group of local charities.

❑ Have a high-profile internal creative award, the winners chosen by expert external judges.

❑ Have a self-deprecating, satirical, fun firm magazine.

❑ Have ad-hoc events like firmwide parties and open days.

❑ Keep doing things that surprise people.

❑ Laugh at their mistakes and kid each other.

❑ Offer free massages, shoeshines, book clubs, exercise classes, language lessons, surprise ice cream sundaes, pinball machines, gifts on Mother's Day, and so on.

❏ Arrange office outings to film premieres, gigs and shows.
❏ Announce promotions in song.
❏ Announce the top ten mistakes of the year.
❏ Provide a budget to decorate meeting rooms for regular office meetings.
❏ Hold a parents' day: Let people bring their kids to work.
❏ Fund client entertainment liberally.
❏ Make work as pleasant as possible because that is where you spend the most time!
❏ Regularly throw a good party! This can retain people and increase billability by 15 percent!
❏ Work hard with their people and play hard. People like and need a release.

CHAPTER TWENTY-THREE

Lessons: Other Topics

Hiring

We heard a lot about hiring, and a lot of it is central to the culture that these top managers were trying to create. Here's what they advise:

- ❑ Don't hire just anybody. Have a sense of who is and who is not your firm's kind of person. Hire to fit the culture. Wait and get the right person.
- ❑ Hire people with enthusiasm, excitement, sparks, energy, spirit, a sharing style, smarts, personality, compatibility and vision.
- ❑ Look for a cooperative spirit; a dedication to teamwork; a service mentality; a non-argumentative attitude.
- ❑ Try to hire people who have all this innate in their personality.
- ❑ In recruiting, ask questions like "What kind of people do you like to work for? What kind of people do you like working for you?" "What type of place do you like?"
- ❑ Involve the whole team in hiring.
- ❑ Do investment hiring, taking the risk of hiring in advance of demand.
- ❑ Treat recruitment interviews more as a pitch process, not an exam.

❏ Have inductions in which everyone who joins is assigned a "buddy" or mentor who makes sure the new recruit meets everyone and understands how everything works.

❏ Have new-hire lunches.

❏ When you hire, be absolutely honest about what your firm can offer.

Training

As we have seen in our statistics and in our case studies, training may not be a primary driver, but it clearly plays an essential support role. Here's what to do, according to those who've been there and done it:

❏ Allow anyone to take anything in training they want as long as it is somehow related to the business.

❏ Allow people to select their own training, with full tuition reimbursement.

❏ Don't cancel training if profits are down.

❏ Encourage everyone to take two courses per year.

❏ Give a stipend to each person to use for training purposes. Talk to them if they fail to use it.

❏ Have a professional training program, but place the emphasis on lots of mentoring.

❏ Have in-house training, your own "college."

❏ Hold "Doctor Is In" sessions, where any team can bring in a problem they are having. For 15 minutes the "doctors" do "fast brainstorming."

❏ Hold a "Lunch and Learn" series of miniworkshops.

❏ Hold coaching programs regularly.

❏ Hold formal on-site as well as off-site training programs.

❏ Hold managerial training (people management) for managers at all levels.

❑ If a person says, "I can't make the seminar because of a client conflict," call the client and say, "My person needs to do this; can I fill in or make other arrangements?"

❑ Interpret training liberally (acting lessons, voice coach).

❑ Listen to employee input and adjust training programs.

❑ Of all your training about 80 percent should be about personal development and only 20 percent technical training.

❑ Offer courses on handling conflicts, anger management.

❑ Run training courses like a college, all voluntary.

❑ Send forms out to identify training needs of employees and to inquire about any programs that they may know about.

❑ Training works best when insiders do it and they are committed to what they do.

Reward Systems

Next, pay. As we've seen, you've got to get it right. Here are the experts' suggestions on how to do precisely that.

❑ Announce pay decisions in person, in private, one on one.

❑ Base raises on a mix of subjectivity and objectivity.

❑ Create a balanced scorecard for the firm and for individuals' performance.

❑ Ensure your people always know why they got what they got.

❑ Give raises and performance reviews at different times of the year.

❑ Have a pension plan with maximum contribution.

❑ Have everyone sign a confidentiality statement regarding compensation and bonuses, so no one else knows what another person gets.

❑ Have profit sharing, where everyone gets rewarded the same percentage.

❏ Give "spot" bonuses. Each manager should be given a pool at the beginning of the year to use for that purpose.

❏ Tie pay to profitability, but not by formulaic incentives.

❏ Personally review profits with everyone, and discuss what they make and why.

❏ There should be a shared success bonus pool for everyone, based on office results and profitability.

❏ Time bonuses to match performance throughout the year, don't just award at year-end.

Dealing with Clients

The focus of this book has not been about tactics for dealing with clients, but it is not surprising that ways of dealing with clients are integrally connected to how firms are run. Here's what we heard from our case studies:

❏ Aim for a smaller client roster, but with roots deeper in each relationship.

❏ At some point the client will spot any boredom, because you can only cover it up for so long.

❏ Whoever "pitches" the work also does the work.

❏ Be liberal with expenses necessary to entertain clients.

❏ Be willing to confront the client on your people's behalf.

❏ Conduct annual face-to-face client reviews.

❏ Constantly ask people and clients: What do you want?

❏ Do "fun" things with the client.

❏ Do your homework, trying to bring new things to the client on a regular basis.

❏ Encourage client focus: work with the client, play golf, entertain, have dinner.

❏ Focus on long-term relationships with clients, in depth and in length.

❏ Get to know all the departments within your clients' organizations.

❏ Give reasonable deadlines to clients.

❏ Go out and get beat up by the clients the same as your people do.

❏ Have an annual client survey and consistently have at least one face-to-face with each client per year. Then have a feedback session with staff afterwards. Discuss the results and act on them.

❏ If you can't care about this client, don't propose on the work.

❏ Institutionalize management meetings with clients every three or six months to talk about the health of the relationship.

❏ Invite clients to see your offices.

❏ Know intimately the plans of all of your most important clients.

❏ Let clients know that you would jump off a bridge for them!

❏ Make caring about the client a part of your work ethic.

❏ Make it your business to know the past and present situation of the clients.

❏ Never talk down to clients. Or anyone else for that matter.

❏ Offer clients the use of your facilities if they need it.

❏ Pitches (new business proposals) are sold on the basis of relationships.

❏ Play fair with the clients.

❏ Publish aggregate client feedback results internally, and use them when making decisions about bonuses.

❏ Regularly write up the three things that keep you awake at night about each client.

❏ Results of client feedback should be used to help you know how you are doing and help you to do your job.

❏ Socializing is very important if the client wants it!

❏ Spend money to speak with consultants to your clients to find out what is going on with the clients.

❏ Encourage your people to be personal with each other and with the clients they serve.

❏ Stick to your market focus, and don't divert from it.

❏ Tell clients everyone on your team is important and can answer their questions.

❏ When a feedback form comes back from the client, have the team fill out same form, and get back to the client.

❏ While you probably would like to spend more time with clients, when you're the manager it is more important that your people learn how to spend time with the clients.

CHAPTER TWENTY-FOUR

It's Not One or the Other, It's Both!

Back in the 1960s, Robert Blake and Jane Mouton developed a powerful model for management called "The Managerial Grid." The basic lesson for managers was simple; it is not enough to be task-focused, oriented only to getting results. Similarly, they argued, it is not sufficient to have only a people focus, being interested in developing your staff. What you must be, they said, is both.

Wisely, they pointed out that this does not mean "a little of each," or compromising one to achieve the other. The art of management is to be fully committed to (and fully skilled at) both.

This powerful insight was rediscovered and elaborated by Collins and Porras in their book *Built to Last*. They call it "avoiding the Tyranny of the OR, and embracing the Genius of the AND." As they point out, "We're not talking about balance here. 'Balance' implies going to the midpoint, fifty-fifty, half and half. . . . A visionary company doesn't seek simply balance between idealism and profitability; it seeks to be highly idealistic and highly profitable."

Here is a quick summary (Table 24–1) of some of the "Genius of the AND" shown by our superstar managers:

This table doesn't really need a lot of elaboration, since I hope it's self-explanatory. However, one or two items deserve emphasis.

Above all else, this book has tried to show that succeeding in business is not about excellence in pleasing clients, or excellence in exciting your people. It's not a trade-off. The very way that you excel at pleasing clients is to excel at exciting your people. Not one,

Table 24–1: Reinforcing (not Opposing) Forces

Caring about clients	AND	Caring about employees
Task focus	AND	People focus
Business development	AND	People development
Tough	AND	Tender
Being demanding	AND	Being supportive
Making money	AND	Having fun
Work hard	AND	Play hard
Financial rewards	AND	Psychological rewards
Being a manager	AND	Being a human being
Treating people as employees	AND	Treating people as human beings
Deciding with the head	AND	Deciding with the heart
Informing	AND	Listening
Taking care of today	AND	Building for the future
Autonomy	AND	Teamwork
Passion	AND	Compassion
Having good ideas	AND	Having the guts to stick with them

not the other, not even a little of each. You've got to be able to be superb at both to achieve superior financial performance. Done right, these things move together, not in opposition to each other.

Similarly, as Blake and Mouton originally proposed, achieving great things does not mean compromising your ambitions in order to accommodate your people. It means exciting your people to achieve great things. A task focus goes hand in hand at great firms with a people focus.

Note that, according to our structural equation modeling (chapter 7), we know for certain that people development *is* business development. The way you grow a business is to develop your people, energize and excite them and focus them on winning. As Charlie Green (my coauthor on *The Trusted Advisor* notes, it is people development that drives firm development, not the reverse. That's what we've demonstrated with our statistical analysis.

So, how do you grow people? You use the techniques revealed by both our quantitative analysis and our case studies. You employ the basic elements of good coaching (or good parenting) to be both extremely demanding *and* extremely supportive. One without the other is ineffective. You also live the simple principle that you make the most money when your goals are not *just* to make the most money but to have the most fun, as well! You work hard (together) and you play hard (together).

Obviously, Table 24–1 can be used as a powerful diagnostic tool. Ask yourself, or ask your people, how well you are doing on each of those things. Remember, the goal is not achieving a balance between each pair. Achieving superior financial returns requires that you are superb at both!

CHAPTER TWENTY-FIVE

The Courage to Manage

Apart from some creative microtactics, the advice given by the superstar office managers and staff is familiar. Similarly, our statistical investigations have given support and evidence not to surprising conclusions, but to familiar ones.

So what, then, is the issue? Why don't all firms do these things? Pfeffer and Sutton put their finger on the issue in a book entitled *The Knowing-Doing Gap.* Just because people know what to do does not mean they will do it.

In my experience, the single biggest barrier to implementing any strategy is courage. What makes our superstar managers so impressive is not what they are doing, but the fact that they are doing it. Many people (and firms) lack the guts to stick with the plans and goals they have set for themselves. They lack the courage of their own convictions. As C. S. Lewis wrote in *The Screw Tape Letters,* "Courage is not simply one of the virtues, but the form of every virtue at the testing point."

I first learned this lesson some time ago, when I set for myself the goal of trying to become a strategic advisor to international professional firms. Shortly thereafter a firm asked me to accept a project conducting sales and marketing training courses for their people.

The assignment was very attractive: a large volume of familiar, comfortable, enjoyable work, which would provide a significant portion of my revenue target for the year. However, it was obvious that spending most of my year doing sales skills training would do nothing to help me achieve my strategic goal. Rather than becoming a strategic advisor, I would, by the end of that year, be a sales trainer.

Taking the expedient path would not have been immoral, but it would have meant that I would not have obtained the benefits of my declared strategy. Obviously, resisting the expedient path is hard. You have to really bet on yourself and believe your own vision. You have to have the courage of your own convictions. Believing in the benefits of your aspirational goals is one thing; living by the diets that are necessary to achieve those goals is another.

So which did I want? Easy cash, or an ambitious strategy that would require hard work to create? Did I want a comfortable, well-paid year or one where I had to accept the burden of generating an equivalent number of days of "real" work that would move me toward my strategic goal as well as generate income? I decided to stick with my strategy and pass on the "easy money" opportunity. I arranged for a friend to look after my client, and worked hard (and successfully) to bring in the kind of work that was "on strategy."

Situations like these are not unusual. In fact, they are *inevitable*. All strategies, at some time or the other, involve a trade-off between short-term cash (doing what's expedient) and executing the strategy (living the vision of excellence you have set for yourself). If you're going to pursue a strategy, you must be willing to make hard choices and act as if you truly believe in your own strategy. In short, executing a strategy takes courage. You must be willing to practice what you preach, when it is convenient and (most importantly) when it is not.

Most firms do a good job of figuring out what needs to be done to improve the firm's success. Drawers and shelves are stuffed with clever plans, strategies and action items that, *if implemented*, would significantly improve the firm's success. However, the hard part of strategy is not coming up with clever ideas. Rather, the difficult part is finding the discipline, the will and the determination to act as if you were serious when you outlined your strategy.

Business life is filled with daily temptations, short-term expediencies and wonderful excuses why we can't afford to execute our strategy today. Accordingly, that new article never gets written, work is delegated only when it must be (not when it can be), the junior staff remains only "adequately" supervised, and the marketing principle is "We never met a dollar of revenue we didn't like!"

There is absolutely nothing wrong about making this choice, but you must not fool yourself. If you are willing to sacrifice a few degrees of quality to earn more cash, you will not create the market reputation for superior quality that you say you seek. It takes courage to believe that a reputation for excellence is worth more in the long run than incremental current cash. In their vision, mission and strategy documents, most firms *say* that they are aiming for excellence, but that's not how they operate.

In describing this trade-off in one firm, a person asked, "Are you really saying we should turn down new business?" "Only if you don't have the capacity to do it to high standards," I replied. "But does anyone ever do that?" she inquired. "Only the most profitable firms," I replied. "We wouldn't have the courage to do that," she said. "Precisely," I replied, "You don't actually have the courage to believe your own mission, vision and strategy." "Oh, I do," she said, "But I don't believe that our firm management does."

There lies the real difference between the average firm and the superstar offices described in this book. They don't preach standards that are different; they just live those standards. And the reason they do is not found in clever systems, but in the strength of the convictions of the individual managers who run those offices.

Many people do not believe that their leaders truly want them to act strategically. Whenever there is a choice to be made between strategy and short-term cash (and there always is) most people feel under significant (if not irresistible) pressure from management to go for the cash.

They believe that the message from firm leadership is clear: Strategy can wait for tomorrow. Rather than firm leadership being a source of encouragement to stay the course and pull off the strategy, they all too often *are* the biggest obstacles to the implementation of strategy. The courage to bet on the articulated strategy, even when it is management's own strategy, is almost entirely lacking.

The principle of courage is not meant to be an inspirational point, but simple logic. You reap the benefits of what you actually do, not what you hope to get around to doing some day if it is convenient and you're not too busy. If you want to be known as excellent at something then you have to *be* reliably, consistently excellent at that thing.

One could argue that you don't have to be "slavish" about your strategy. For example, couldn't you *occasionally* take in too much work, as long as overall you were excellent? This is a tempting argument, but in the real world it fails for two reasons. First, once you start forgiving yourself a little ("just this once") it is remarkable how easy it is to find reasons to forgive yourself for being expedient the next time (and the next, and the next . . .). Before you know it, your standards are no longer standards, and are just aspirations.

Secondly, the harsh reality of marketplaces is that it is very hard to develop a reputation for excellence for something that you do "most of the time." Even if you depart from excellence only a few times, you quickly become known as inconsistent or unreliable. If you can't be depended upon, few buyers will single you out as special.

Many people believe that you can rely on reward systems to encourage the implementation of strategy. This is rarely true. Take, for example, the strategy of excellence in managing people, an approach to doing business which is ardently preached in most firms and rarely enforced. "Well, we pay attention to it, it's one of our key strategies" one of my clients said. "We reward those people who do it well." "And what do you do to those people who don't do it well?" I asked. "We just don't reward them," he replied.

"In other words, you allow them to carry on as before?" I commented. "Well, yes," he said. "In other words, they don't have to do it, if they don't want to?" I queried. "I suppose not," he said. "Then how many do it?" I asked. "A few," he admitted. "So you're not achieving firmwide excellence in this area?" I concluded. "Not really, I suppose," he said.

The lesson is clear. To make something happen, it's not enough to reward those who choose to participate. You must tackle those who do not. As long as it's optional (even if rewarded) it isn't going to be done at the level at which the commercial benefits will kick in. "Are you really saying that I need to speak with all those who aren't doing it?" he asked. "Only if you want the benefits of your declared strategy," I replied.

"I'm not suggesting that you play boss, cop, Attila the Hun or dictator. Go remind them of why you chose that strategy. Help them. Encourage them. Give them some tools to make it easier. Set targets for small improvements that will at least get them on the virtuous path. But whatever you do, don't ignore them or leave them alone. It's not a standard in your firm if there are no consequences for noncompliance."

"But it would take an enormous amount of emotional energy to do all that," he said.

"Welcome to the wonderful world of managing," I said.

Many managers believe that they add their greatest value in ensuring that a strategy (or vision, or mission, or direction) is developed. However, this is patently false. The greatest value of a leader is in ensuring that the strategy is *implemented.* This is revealed by the very origin of the word "manage" which derives from Old French and, literally translated, means "the holder of horses." The manager's key role is to ensure that all the horses are moving in the agreed-upon direction at approximately the same pace.

Over the years, I have been trusted to see the strategic plans of many direct competitors. Remarkably, they are almost always identical. Everyone figures out correctly which client sectors are growing, which services are in rising demand, and which dimensions of competition (client service, innovation, etc.) the clients are looking for. The strategy documents are the same not because people are being dumb, but for precisely the opposite reason: everyone's smart! Everyone knows what needs to be done.

If this is so, then what is competition really all about? In my experience, it is about who can best *get done* the (obvious) things that need to get done. And this, in turn, is determined by the following set of closely related concepts:

- ❑ Energy
- ❑ Drive
- ❑ Enthusiasm
- ❑ Excitement
- ❑ Passion
- ❑ Ambition

Where these exist, the discipline can be found to engage in diligent execution and thereby outperform the competition.

The role of the manager, then, is to be a net creator of enthusiasm, excitement, passion and ambition. Any manager who can create these things will launch the "Service Profit Chain" that Heskett and colleagues wrote about so convincingly.

Alas, all too often, managers are net destroyers of excitement. If all they ever talk about is finances ("How are your billings, what's happening to receivables?") it can be deadening to the spirit. Which doesn't mean they don't need to talk about these things. They do. However, they must not talk *only* about these things. Financial discipline is the bedrock of business success. It is not all of it.

It is the manager's job not only to manage financials, but to inspire, cajole, exhort, nag, support, critique, praise, encourage, confront and comfort as individual people (and groups of people) struggle to live their work lives according to new standards—that is, the strategy. Of all the qualities required of managers, the most essential is courage—the courage actually to manage, and enforce the standards that are preached.

Managers must have the courage to maintain a long-term focus, must retain the courage of the convictions they espouse, and must find the courage to intervene personally whenever there are departures from the values and vision that create excellence.

The single biggest problem in the implementation of strategies is the absence of "consequences for noncompliance." If the manager doesn't have the courage to tackle the individual who is not behaving in accordance with the strategy, then all the other people will quickly realize that the new strategy is not something you *have* to do. They will quickly cease *striving* to comply. And thus the benefits of the strategy will never be attained. The single question remains: "What is the manager going to do about noncompliance?" Hundreds, if not thousands, of eyes are watching closely to see if the announced strategies are real or are discretionary.

What is often underestimated is that the problem of the nonconforming person is not his or her own nonparticipation in the strategy, but the adverse effect that he or she has on the motivation of others to participate in the new initiatives.

Afraid to intervene, many managers wait until the problems become serious. Until they *have* to deal with them. It is, after all, emotionally easier to deal with problems only when you must. This is, however, insufficient. Managing is not about dealing with problems once they have become unavoidable. Rather, managing is about surfacing issues and dealing with them *before* they become problems. To make a new strategy work, the manager needs to demonstrate, visibly, that he or she is prepared to be intolerant about departures from the strategy.

The earlier you deal with problems, the easier it is to tackle them, and the more options you have. The most obvious "consequence for noncompliance" should be an informal, unscheduled, private office visit from the manager. "Mary, it's come to my attention that you're not participating in the team meetings that we agreed to have. Is this accurate? Is there a problem? Is there something I can help you with?" (As always in managing, the best strategy is to describe the situation and ask for an explanation first.)

If the person is reluctant to go along, it is possible to ask for help:

"Fred, I know this isn't something that you enjoy, or that someone with your skills needs, but I really want to help and encourage others in this area, and your participation would carry enormous weight. Would you do it as a favor for me?"

Having these conversations is never easy, and takes significant interpersonal skill, particularly when the problem is not yet a serious one. But that's what managing is! While skill is involved, courage is even more essential. More managers have the skill to conduct these conversations than have the courage to actually engage in them. The manager is never adding as much value as when he or she is influencing individuals to adhere to agreed upon actions. Managing is less about figuring what should happen, than it is about actually making it happen.

It should be clear that the more the word gets out that noncompliance will result in an office visit from the manager, the less often the manager will need to make those visits. People will stay in compliance just to keep you out of their office!

A successful manager must not only have the courage to manage; he or she must also have the ability to instill courage in others. The central problem in most firms is that things are "pretty good so far." Few firms are hurting badly. And, as the old saying goes, the good is the enemy of the best. Why bother stretching for excellence when things are (at least) acceptable as they are. Do I really want to suffer the rigors of a new diet in order to achieve the uncertain benefits of a new goal? Or, in summary, do we really have to do this?

It is often said that only two things motivate people, fear and greed. Yet there has been very little reference to either of those things in this book. The best managers make use of a third motivating force, the glamorous dream. They are able to convince their colleagues that life could indeed be significantly better, that greater accomplishment is possible, and that, yes, they can do it.

Great managers give their people the confidence to believe that, individually and collectively, success, fulfillment, accomplishment and profits are, indeed, attainable. They give them the courage to try.

Change poses threat, and many if not most people operate well within their comfort zone, but are reluctant to abandon the old habits that brought them to their current level of success. If managers are often demanding, they must also be supportive. They must manage with a style that sends the signal "Come on, you can do it, I will help you!"

While the first part of this message ("Come on") is common enough, the second two, personal encouragement and personal support, are often absent in the styles of many managers. Again, it is necessary to notice that doing this kind of one-on-one management (the only form of management worthy of the name) takes not only skill but also the courage to actually do it.

Just as management involves a delicate balance between being supportive and being demanding, it also requires a style of insistent patience. Patience that "Rome doesn't get built in a day," and insistence that "We *are* building Rome." To find the courage to keep trying to attain new levels of performance, people must believe in their heart of hearts that the manager actually does believe what he or she says about the firm's standards, mission, vision and strategies.

People must believe that the manager has the courage to believe in something and, more importantly, the guts to stick with it. There is no greater condemnation of a manager than to say that he or she is expedient, and no greater commendation than to say that he or she truly lives and acts in accordance with what he or she preaches.

The Financial Performance Index

The financial performance index is made up of four underlying measures:

1. Profit margin
2. Profit per employee
3. Two-year growth in revenues
4. Two-year growth in profits

The purpose of this brief appendix is to reveal how much the index is dependent on each of these measures. The table below shows the strength of the correlation between each measure and the financial performance index, using the "R-squared" statistic. The R-squared measure shows the percentage of the variation in one variable that can be "explained" or "accounted for" by changes in the other variable. Thus changes in profit per employee seem to "explain" 53 percent of all the variation in the financial performance index, whereas the differences in the margin measure can account for "only" 24 percent of the differences among offices in the financial performance index.

As the table shows, the strongest correlations with the financial index occur with the two-year growth in profit and the profit per employee. These two financial figures seem to drive the overall index score slightly more than the other two financial measures, though all show a significant statistical relationship with the overall FPI score.

Percent of variation in financial performance index that can be explained by these factors (R-squared)	
Profit growth	.81
Profit per employee	.53
Revenue growth	.27
Margin	.24

All these correlations are statistically significant at the .01 level.

What these statistics show is that the financial performance index does a fairly good job of combining (and representing) the underlying four measures. All four influence the index (to varying degrees).

The 74 questions

Here are the overall results for the entire set of 139 offices, with three numbers (on our scale of 1 to 6) given for each question:

- ❏ The first quartile (Q1) shows the score exceeded by 75 percent of the respondents, and which exceeds the score given by 25 percent of respondents.
- ❏ The median (M) shows the "middle point," the score exceeded by 50 percent of respondents and which exceeds the score given by the other 50 percent of the respondents.
- ❏ The third quartile (Q3) shows the score exceeded by only 25 percent of the respondents, and which exceeds the score given by 75 percent of the respondents.

Using these results, you could survey your own office(s) and benchmark your firm against this database. I have arranged the questions in descending order of the score on the median (average).

Statement	Q1	M	Q3
1. We make our clients feel as if they're important to us.	4.9	5.1	5.3
2. Client satisfaction is a top priority at our firm.	4.7	5.0	5.2

(continued)

Statement	Q1	M	Q3
3. I can generally decide for myself the best way to get my work done.	4.8	5.0	5.1
4. The quality of work performed for clients by my group is consistently high.	4.6	4.9	5.1
5. We do a good job of resolving client problems when they occur.	4.7	4.9	5.0
6. We listen well to what the client has to say.	4.6	4.8	5.0
7. The quality of service delivered to clients by my group is consistently high.	4.6	4.8	5.0
8. Most people in our office do "whatever it takes" to do a good job for their clients.	4.4	4.7	4.9
9. We would rather be the best than the biggest.	4.3	4.7	5.0
10. I have the freedom to make the necessary decisions to do my work properly.	4.4	4.7	4.9
11. Our team is effective at achieving our desired results.	4.4	4.6	4.8
12. When necessary, people put the needs of the office ahead of their own.	4.3	4.6	4.8
13. We keep clients informed on issues affecting their business.	4.3	4.6	4.9

Statement	Q1	M	Q3
14. We constantly strive to find innovative solutions to clients' problems.	4.3	4.6	4.8
15. This is a very demanding place to work.	4.2	4.6	4.8
16. I often express my views on issues important to me, even when I know that others will disagree.	4.4	4.5	4.7
17. We have a real commitment to high levels of client service, and tolerate nothing else.	4.2	4.5	4.8
18. I am actively encouraged to volunteer new ideas and make suggestions for improvement of our business.	4.1	4.5	4.8
19. We are extremely good at building long-term client relationships.	4.2	4.5	4.8
20. We have a real commitment to high quality work, and tolerate nothing less.	4.2	4.5	4.7
21. People here enjoy interacting with clients: We're not just interested in the work we do for them.	4.2	4.5	4.7
22. In this office we set and enforce very high standards for performance.	4.1	4.4	4.7
23. We consistently work well as a team.	4.1	4.4	4.6

(continued)

Statement	Q1	M	Q3
24. I am committed to this firm as a career opportunity.	4.2	4.4	4.6
25. I am a member of a well-functioning team.	4.0	4.4	4.6
26. This is a fun place to work.	3.9	4.4	4.7
27. Our management values inputs from all levels.	4.0	4.3	4.7
28. The actions of our firm are consistent with our strategic objectives and mission statement.	4.1	4.3	4.6
29. We always place the clients' interests first, ahead of those of the office.	4.1	4.3	4.5
30. We have an uncompromising determination to achieve excellence in everything we do.	4.0	4.3	4.6
31. I often talk to my superiors about any concerns I might have about my work.	4.0	4.3	4.6
32. I get a great sense of accomplishment from my work.	4.1	4.3	4.5
33. People are more dedicated here than in most other organizations.	3.9	4.3	4.6
34. The quality of the professionals in our office is as high as can be expected.	3.8	4.2	4.6

Statement	Q1	M	Q3
35. The emphasis in our office is on long-term success, rather than short-term results.	3.9	4.2	4.6
36. My manager is more a coach than a boss	3.8	4.1	4.5
37. Poor performance is not tolerated here.	3.8	4.1	4.4
38. We are focused as a team on specific team goals.	3.9	4.1	4.4
39. Management operates in accordance with the firm's overall philosophy and values: they practice what they preach.	3.8	4.1	4.6
40. People within our office always treat others with respect.	3.6	4.1	4.4
41. Management around here is trusted.	3.6	4.1	4.5
42. I am highly satisfied with my job.	3.8	4.0	4.3
43. We maintain a balance between short- and long-term goals.	3.7	4.0	4.3
44. The quality of supervision on client projects is uniformly high.	3.7	4.0	4.2
45. There are real opportunities here for meaningful career and professional advancement.	3.8	4.0	4.4

(continued)

Statement	Q1	M	Q3
46. My immediate manager is an extremely effective coach.	3.7	4.0	4.3
47. I am given the chance at the office to learn and develop new skills.	3.7	4.0	4.3
48. The management of our office always listens to our people.	3.5	4.0	4.3
49. We have a strong culture. If you don't fit in, you won't make it here.	3.7	4.0	4.3
50. The overwhelming majority of the work I'm given is challenging rather than repetitive.	3.7	3.9	4.2
51. We invest a significant amount of time in things that will pay off in the future.	3.7	3.9	4.2
52. Communication between the office's management and people at my level is very good.	3.5	3.9	4.2
53. Management of our office is successful in fostering commitment and loyalty.	3.4	3.9	4.3
54. I know exactly what my office is trying to achieve strategically.	3.5	3.9	4.3
55. We make unusual efforts to identify and recruit the best people for every job.	3.6	3.9	4.3

Statement	Q1	M	Q3
56. We do a good job of delegating work to the appropriate level.	3.6	3.9	4.1
57. Considering my contribution, I think I am paid fairly compared to others in the office.	3.6	3.8	4.1
58. We regularly discuss the results of client satisfaction feedback.	3.5	3.8	4.2
59. Those who contribute the most to the overall success of the office are the most highly rewarded.	3.5	3.8	4.2
60. We have no room for those who put their personal agenda ahead of the interests of the clients or the office.	3.5	3.8	3.9
61. We regularly discuss our progress toward our strategic objectives, not just the financial goals.	3.4	3.7	4.1
62. The amount of work I have keeps me challenged, but not overwhelmed.	3.5	3.7	3.9
63. Around here you are required, not just encouraged, to learn and develop new skills.	3.3	3.7	4.1
64. We emphasize teamwork here. Individualistic people aren't tolerated.	3.4	3.7	4.0

(continued)

Statement	Q1	M	Q3
65. We keep our people informed about what is happening in the office.	3.2	3.6	4.1
66. Management gets the best work out of everybody in the office.	3.4	3.6	4.0
67. Considering the office as a whole, the compensation system is managed equitably and fairly.	3.3	3.6	3.9
68. This place has done a good job of providing the training I've needed to do my job well.	3.3	3.6	4.0
69. There is more opportunity to move ahead rapidly here than is possible at most other places.	3.2	3.6	4.0
70. We have an effective system in place to measure client feedback.	3.2	3.6	4.0
71. Management shows by their actions that employee training is important.	3.0	3.5	4.0
72. I am actively helped with my personal development.	3.1	3.3	3.7
73. We have high-quality training opportunities to improve skills.	2.7	3.1	3.7
74. Enthusiasm and morale around here have never been higher.	2.5	2.9	3.5

The Factors

As explained in the text, factors are question groups determined by a statistical technique called factor analysis. This technique examines the correlations between questions, and forms the groups (without human intervention) based on an analysis of which clusters of questions tended to receive similar responses; that is, the responses to the questions within the group tended to move in synchronization with each other.

While I did not choose the clusters, I did name them. Feel free to substitute better summary names if you can identify them.

The nine factors here can account for 68 percent of all the variation in the 74 questions.

Factor 1: Quality and client relationships

❑ We make our clients feel as if they're important to us.
❑ We keep clients informed on issues affecting their business.
❑ We have a real commitment to high levels of client service, and tolerate nothing else.
❑ Client satisfaction is a top priority at our firm.
❑ The quality of work performed for clients by my group is consistently high.
❑ We are extremely good at building long-term client relationships.

❑ The quality of service delivered to clients by my group is consistently high.

❑ Most people in our office do "whatever it takes" to do a good job for their clients.

❑ We do a good job of resolving client problems when they occur.

❑ We listen well to what the client has to say.

❑ We have a real commitment to high-quality work, and tolerate nothing less.

❑ We always place the clients' interests first, ahead of those of the office.

Factor 2: Training and Development

❑ This place has done a good job of providing the training I've needed to do my job well.

❑ I am actively helped with my personal development.

❑ Around here you are required, not just encouraged, to learn and develop new skills.

❑ Management shows by their actions that employee training is important.

❑ We have high-quality training opportunities to improve skills.

❑ I am given the chance at the office to learn and develop new skills.

Factor 3: Coaching

❑ My manager is more a coach than a boss.

❑ My immediate manager is an extremely effective coach.

❑ I often talk to my superiors about any concerns I might have about my work.

❑ I am a member of a well-functioning team.

Factor 4: Commitment, Enthusiasm and Respect

❑ Enthusiasm and morale around here have never been higher.
❑ Management of our office is successful in fostering commitment and loyalty.
❑ This is a fun place to work.
❑ People within our office always treat others with respect.
❑ We have no room for those who put their individual interests ahead of the interests of the clients or the office.
❑ Management gets the best work out of everybody in the office.

Factor 5: High Standards

❑ The quality of the professionals in our office is as high as can be expected.
❑ Poor performance is not tolerated here.
❑ This is a very demanding place to work.
❑ When necessary, people put the needs of the office ahead of their own.
❑ We have a strong culture. If you don't fit in, you won't make it here.

Factor 6: Long-Term Orientation

❑ I know exactly what my office is trying to achieve strategically.
❑ We maintain a balance between short- and long-term goals.
❑ We regularly discuss our progress toward our strategic objectives, not just the financial goals.
❑ We invest a significant amount of time in things that will pay off in the future.
❑ The emphasis in our office is on long-term success, rather than short-term results.

Factor 7: Empowerment

❏ I am actively encouraged to volunteer new ideas and make suggestions for improvement of our business.
❏ I have the freedom to make the necessary decisions to do my work properly.
❏ I often express my views on issues important to me, even when I know that others will disagree.
❏ I can generally decide for myself the best way to get my work done.

Factor 8: Fair Compensation

❏ Those who contribute the most to the overall success of the office are the most highly rewarded.
❏ Considering my contribution, I think I am paid fairly compared to others in the office.
❏ Considering the office as a whole, the compensation system is managed equitably and fairly.

Factor 9: Employee Satisfaction

❏ I am highly satisfied with my job.
❏ I get a great sense of accomplishment from my work.
❏ The overwhelming majority of the work I'm given is challenging rather than repetitive.
❏ I am committed to this firm as a career opportunity.

Impact of Improving on Each Question

Another way to explore the relationship between attitudes and financial performance, not shown in the main text of this book, is to ask, "Did offices that scored high on a particular question tend to have a higher financial performance index (FPI) than those that scored relatively low on that question?"

The results are striking. All but ten of the questions showed greater than a 20 percent financial advantage for the offices scoring highest on that question.

Just to be clear on what was done, let's review the result for the first question in the table below. The 20 percent of all offices that scored highest on "We listen well to what the client has to say" averaged a score on the question that was 10 percent higher than the average of the remaining 80 percent of the offices. Examining the financial performance of the same set of offices that scored highest *on this question*, it was discovered that they achieved (on average) a 67 percent higher financial performance index (FPI) than the remaining 80 percent of offices did.

Comparing the 10 percent improvement in question response with the 67 percent improvement in financial result, we could say that improvements on this question have a multiple of 6.7.

Following this logic, here are the twenty questions with the biggest multiples.

	Percent Improvement in Survey Question	Percent Improvement in FPI	Multiple
1. We listen well to what the client has to say.	10	67	6.7
2. We always place the clients' interests first, ahead of those of the office.	12	79	6.6
3. Our team is effective at achieving our desired results.	12	78	6.5
4. We keep clients informed on issues affecting their business.	14	80	5.5
5. We consistently work well as a team.	15	85	5.5
6. I often talk to my superiors about any concerns I might have about my work.	16	82	5.0
7. I get a great sense of accomplishment from my work.	14	66	4.8
8. In this office we set and enforce very high standards for performance.	20	90	4.6

	Percent	Percent	Multiple
9. I am highly satisfied with my job.	16	71	4.6
10. We make our clients feel as if they're important to us.	10	47	4.5
11. I am committed to this firm as a career opportunity.	16	70	4.5
12. The quality of service delivered to clients by my group is consistently high.	11	48	4.3
13. The quality of supervision on client projects is uniformly high.	15	57	3.9
14. This is a fun place to work.	21	79	3.7
15. I can generally decide for myself the best way to get my work done.	9.5	36	3.7
16. We have a real commitment to high levels of client service, and tolerate nothing else.	17	64	3.7
17. The quality of the professionals in our office is as high as can be expected.	22	82	3.7

(continued)

	Percent	Percent	Multiple
18. We do a good job of resolving client problems when they occur.	9	33	3.6
19. The quality of work performed for clients by my group is consistently high.	12	45	3.6
20. We have a real commitment to high-quality work, and tolerate nothing less.	15	54	3.5

As the table shows, a relatively small difference in performance on the individual questions (from 10 to 28 percent) corresponds with a relatively large difference in the FPI (from 64 to 90 percent).

Comparison of the Nine Factors

The results of improving on each of the nine factors show that a relatively small change in a factor's score is coupled with a significant difference in the FPI. The greatest amount of impact on the index is in quality and client relationships (only an 11 percent difference in the assessment scores, but almost 86 percent disparity in the FPI). Fair compensation also shows a large impact.

	Percent Improvement in Factor	Percent Improvement in FPI	Multiple
Quality and client relationships	11	86	8.0
Fair compensation	19	84	4.3
Coaching	16	63	4.0
High standards	15	59	3.9
Employee satisfaction & morale	13	42	3.2
Empowerment	11	32	2.9
Commitment, enthusiasm and respect	24	63	2.6
Long-term orientation	18	40	2.3
Training and development	27	29	1.1

How the Top 20 Percent Offices Did It

Scores in this table show the percentage increase in answers to the survey question that was achieved by the 20 percent of offices that were most financially successful over the average of the remaining 80 percent of offices.

Said another way: The average of the scores given by employees at the most financially successful offices on the question "Enthusiasm and morale around here have never been higher" was 15 percent higher than the average of the scores given by employees at the less financially successful offices.

Question	Percent Difference
1. Enthusiasm and morale around here have never been higher.	15
2. Management gets the best work out of everybody in the office.	12
3. Management of our office is successful in fostering commitment and loyalty.	12

Question	Percent Difference

4. The management of our office always listens to our people. — 12

5. People are more dedicated here than in most other organizations. — 12

6. Considering the office as a whole, the compensation system is managed equitably and fairly. — 11

7. Management around here is trusted. — 11

8. The quality of the professionals in our office is as high as can be expected. — 11

9. Management operates in accordance with the firm's overall philosophy and values; they practice what they preach. — 10

10. Those who contribute the most to the overall success of the office are the most highly rewarded. — 10

11. Communication between the office's management and people at my level is very good. — 10

12. We would rather be the best than the biggest. — 9

13. In this office we set and enforce very high standards for performance. — 9

(continued)

Question	Percent Difference
14. Most people in our office do "whatever it takes" to do a good job for their clients.	9
15. We have a real commitment to high levels of client service, and tolerate nothing else.	9
16. We invest a significant amount of time in things that will pay off in the future.	9
17. We regularly discuss our progress toward our strategic objectives, not just the financial goals.	9
18. Our management values inputs from all levels.	8
19. People within our office always treat others with respect.	8
20. My manager is more a coach than a boss.	8
21. The emphasis in our office is on long-term success, rather than short-term results.	8
22. We make unusual efforts to identify and recruit the best people for every job.	8
23. We have a real commitment to high-quality work, and tolerate nothing less.	8
24. I am actively encouraged to volunteer new ideas and make suggestions for improvement of our business.	8

Question	Percent Difference
25. We have an uncompromising determination to achieve excellence in everything we do.	8
26. Considering my contribution, I think I am paid fairly compared to others in the office.	7
27. There are real opportunities here for meaningful career and professional advancement.	7
28. We keep clients informed on issues affecting their business.	7
29. I am committed to this firm as a career opportunity.	7
30. We consistently work well as a team.	7
31. There is more opportunity to move ahead rapidly here than is possible at most other places.	7
32. We maintain a balance between short- and long-term goals.	7
33. Our team is effective at achieving our desired results.	7
34. This is a fun place to work.	7
35. We have high-quality training opportunities to improve skills.	7

(continued)

Question	Percent Difference
36. We emphasize teamwork here. Individualistic people aren't tolerated.	7
37. We constantly strive to find innovative solutions to clients' problems.	6
38. The quality of work performed for clients by my group is consistently high.	6
39. The quality of service delivered to clients by my group is consistently high.	6
40. We regularly discuss the results of client satisfaction feedback.	6
41. We do a good job of delegating work to the appropriate level.	6
42. I am highly satisfied with my job.	6
43. I get a great sense of accomplishment from my work.	6
44. We always place the clients' interests first, ahead of those of the office.	6
45. My immediate manager is an extremely effective coach.	6
46. Client satisfaction is a top priority at our firm.	6
47. The quality of supervision on client projects is uniformly high.	6

Question	Percent Difference
48. We keep our people informed about what is happening in the office.	6
49. We listen well to what the client has to say.	5
50. Poor performance is not tolerated here.	5
51. The actions of our firm are consistent with our strategic objectives and mission statement.	5
52. We are extremely good at building long-term client relationships.	5
53. We are focused as a team on specific team goals.	5
54. The overwhelming majority of the work I'm given is challenging rather than repetitive.	5
55. We have no room for those who put their personal agenda ahead of the interests of the clients or the office.	5
56. This place has done a good job of providing the training I've needed to do my job well.	5
57. When necessary, people put the needs of the office ahead of their own.	5
58. I have the freedom to make the necessary decisions to do my work properly.	5

(continued)

Question	Percent Difference
59. We do a good job of resolving client problems when they occur.	4
60. We make our clients feel as if they're important to us.	4
61. The amount of work I have keeps me challenged, but not overwhelmed.	4
62. Management shows by their actions that employee training is important. *	4
63. I am given the chance at the office to learn and develop new skills.	4
64. I know exactly what my office is trying to achieve strategically.	4
65. I am a member of a well-functioning team.	4
66. I am actively helped with my personal development.	4
67. We have a strong culture. If you don't fit in, you won't make it here.	4
68. People here enjoy interacting with clients: we're not just interested in the work we do for them.	4
69. I often talk to my superiors about any concerns I might have about my work.	4

Question	Percent Difference
70. We have an effective system in place to measure client feedback.*	2
71. I can generally decide for myself the best way to get my work done.	2
72. Around here you are required, not just encouraged, to learn and develop new skills.*	1
73. This is a very demanding place to work.*	0
74. I often express my views on issues important to me, even when I know that others will disagree.*	0

*Difference is not statistically significant. All other results are.

Correlations

The table below shows the percent of variation in financial performance that can be explained by each of the questions in the survey (r-squared).

Question	Percent
1. We have an uncompromising determination to achieve excellence in everything we do.	23
2. We have a real commitment to high levels of client service, and tolerate nothing else.	22
3. In this office we set and enforce very high standards for performance.	21
4. Client satisfaction is a top priority at our firm.	21
5. We listen well to what the client has to say.	21
6. Our team is effective at achieving our desired results.	20

Question	Percent
7. We keep clients informed on issues affecting their business.	20
8. We have a real commitment to high-quality work, and tolerate nothing less.	19
9. The quality of work performed for clients by my group is consistently high.	19
10. We maintain a balance between short- and long-term goals.	18
11. The quality of service delivered to clients by my group is consistently high.	17
12. Those who contribute the most to the overall success of the office are the most highly rewarded.	17
13. We invest a significant amount of time in things that will pay off in the future.	17
14. We make our clients feel as if they're important to us.	17
15. Management gets the best work out of everybody in the office.	16
16. The emphasis in our office is on long-term success, rather than short-term results.	16
17. I am committed to this firm as a career opportunity.	16

(continued)

Question	Percent
18. The actions of our firm are consistent with our strategic objectives and mission statement.	15
19. There are real opportunities here for meaningful career and professional advancement.	15
20. The quality of the professionals in our office is as high as can be expected.	14
21. We do a good job of resolving client problems when they occur.	13
22. The management of our office always listens to our people.	13
23. Management of our office is successful in fostering commitment and loyalty.	13
24. We consistently work well as a team.	13
25. Management operates in accordance with the firm's overall philosophy and values: They practice what they preach.	12
26. When necessary, people put the needs of the office ahead of their own.	12
27. Most people in our office do "whatever it takes" to do a good job for their clients.	12
28. We do a good job of delegating work to the appropriate level.	11

Question	Percent
29. Considering the office as a whole, the compensation system is managed equitably and fairly.	11
30. We are extremely good at building long-term client relationships.	11
31. People are more dedicated here than in most other organizations.	11
32. My immediate manager is an extremely effective coach.	11
33. We always place the clients' interests first, ahead of those of the office.	10
34. Management around here is trusted.	10
35. We regularly discuss the results of client satisfaction feedback.	10
36. I am a member of a well-functioning team.	10
37. This place has done a good job of providing the training I've needed to do my job well.	9
38. My manager is more a coach than a boss.	9
39. Enthusiasm and morale around here have never been higher.	9

(continued)

Question	Percent
40. Communication between the office's management and people at my level is very good.	8
41. The quality of supervision on client projects is uniformly high.	8
42. There is more opportunity to move ahead rapidly here than is possible at most other places.	8
43. I get a great sense of accomplishment from my work.	8
44. The overwhelming majority of the work I'm given is challenging rather than repetitive.	8
45. We have an effective system in place to measure client feedback.	8
46. Our management values inputs from all levels.	7
47. We would rather be the best than the biggest.	7
48. We constantly strive to find innovative solutions to clients' problems.	7
49. We keep our people informed about what is happening in the office.	7
50. We regularly discuss our progress toward our strategic objectives, not just the financial goals.	7

Question	Percent
51. I am highly satisfied with my job.	7
52. We make unusual efforts to identify and recruit the best people for every job.	6
53. I often talk to my superiors about any concerns I might have about my work.	6
54. I have the freedom to make the necessary decisions to do my work properly.	6
55. We have high-quality training opportunities to improve skills.	6
56. We emphasize teamwork here. Individualistic people aren't tolerated.	6
57. Considering my contribution, I think I am paid fairly compared to others in the office.	6
58. I am actively encouraged to volunteer new ideas and make suggestions for improvement of our business.	6
59. I know exactly what my office is trying to achieve strategically.	5
60. Poor performance is not tolerated here.	5
61. I am given the chance at the office to learn and develop new skills.	5

(continued)

Question	Percent
62. I am actively helped with my personal development.	5
63. This is a fun place to work.	4
64. We are focused as a team on specific team goals.	4
65. Around here you are required, not just encouraged, to learn and develop new skills.	3
66. Management shows by their actions that employee training is important.	3
67. People within our office always treat others with respect.	2
68. People here enjoy interacting with clients: we're not just interested in the work we do for them.	2
69. I can generally decide for myself the best way to get my work done.	2
70. This is a very demanding place to work.	2
71. We have a strong culture. If you don't fit in, you won't make it here.	1
72. We have no room for those who put their personal agenda ahead of the interests of the clients or the office.	1

Question	Percent
73. The amount of work I have keeps me challenged, but not overwhelmed.	1
74. I often express my views on issues important to me, even when I know that others will disagree.	0

Items 1–47 are significant at the 1 percent level.
Items 48–62 are significant at the 5 percent level.
Items 63–74 are not statistically significant.

A Note on Structural Equation Modeling

Structural equation modeling can be summarized as follows:

❏ The analyst specifies a proposed model that describes the (theorized) relationships among a number of variables as being either causal or correlational.

❏ The proposed model is specified as a diagram and a computer program (AMOS) reads the underlying data set.

❏ AMOS uses an iterative procedure to provide estimates of the model's parameters that provide the best fit between the proposed model and the actual data.

❏ The output consists of a variety of measures that allow assessment of how well the proposed model fits the data. It also provides estimates of the parameters and allows hypothesis testing about the statistical significance of the proposed causal and correlational relationships.

❏ Based on an examination of the output, the analyst modifies the model, by finding and removing nonsignificant paths and then retesting. This process is repeated until a good model is found or the analysis is abandoned.

Even though the results of structural equation models are often referred to as "causal modeling" it is important to note that inferring causality is always imprecise. What can be said is that when a causal model fits a set of data it is possible that the proposed causal pattern could explain the results.

There are a number of approaches to judging how well the model fits the data. The table below describes briefly some of the most common measures, the accepted standards for model fit and the results for this model.

Measure	Accepted Standard	Results for Current Model	Conclusions
Goodness of fit index	Greater than .90	.99	Good model fit
Normed fit index	Greater than .90	.99	Good model fit
Comparative fit index	Greater than .90	.99	Good model fit
Mean square error	Less than .1	.085	Good model fit

Further reading on structural equation modeling can be found in Joseph F. Hair et al., *Multivariate Data Analysis,* Fifth Edition, Prentice Hall.

References

Blake, Robert R. and J. S. Mouton, *The Managerial Grid,* Gulf Publishing, 1964.

Buckingham, Marcus and C. Coffman, *First, Break All the Rules,* Simon & Schuster, 1999.

Collins, James C. and J. I. Porras, *Built to Last,* Harpercollins, 1994.

Endlich, Lisa, *Goldman Sachs: The Culture of Success,* Knopf, 1999.

Hair, Joseph F., R. E. Anderson, R. L. Tatham, W. Black, *Multivariate Data Analysis,* Fifth Edition, Prentice Hall College Division, 1998.

Heskett, J. L., W.E. Sasser and L. A. Schlesinger, *The Service Profit Chain,* The Free Press, 1992.

Kaplan, Robert S., and David P. Norton, *The Balanced Scorecard: Translating Strategy into Action,* Harvard Business School Press, 1996.

Kotter, John P. and J. L. Heskett, *Corporate Culture and Performance,* The Free Press, 1992.

Maister, D. H., *Managing the Professional Service Firm,* Free Press, 1993.

Maister, D. H., *True Professionalism,* Free Press, 1997.

Maister, D. H., C. H. Green, R. M. Galford, *The Trusted Advisor,* Free Press, 2000.

Pfeffer, Jeffrey and R. I. Sutton, *The Knowing-Doing Gap,* Harvard Business School Press, 2000.

Acknowledgements

My biggest debt of gratitude for help with this book is obviously to the men and women, at all levels, of the firms that participated in this study. Not only did they allow me to survey them, at inconvenient times for some of them, but they also trusted me with highly confidential financial information. Many of them were generous with their time and experience in granting the interviews reflected in the case studies reported here. I cannot imagine working with a more cooperative, stimulating and nicer group of people.

Success Profiles, Inc. of Bozeman, Montana, handled the processing of the surveys with quality, efficiency and good humor. Eric Gregg, of Northstar Consulting in Bozeman, conducted the analytical work. Eric was everything a professional should be: talented, responsive and a pleasure to work with. Professor Michael Reilly provided immensely valuable input, particularly on the structural equation modeling.

Many friends and clients (often the same person) helped in critiquing earlier drafts of this manuscript. They include Richard Boggon, David Creelman, Charles Green, Brad Koehn, Ray Kotcher, Patrick McKenna, Gerald Riskin, Larry Roslund, and Abram Sarotta. Thanks go to Dan Maher and Dan O'Brien for the Mortimer Ransford case study.

Julie MacDonald O'Leary exceeded her normal substantial contributions to my books. In addition to her usual guidance as to clarity of exposition, flow of logic and appropriate points of emphasis, she was an active participant in conducting (and interpreting) the interviews. I am very fortunate to have been able to work alongside her for my entire consulting career. We have truly been a team.

My wife, Kathy Maister, was, as ever, an essential part of this effort. She listened, she reacted, she encouraged, she cautioned and she created the supportive environment that is essential for any author to keep going. She is my power supply: a continuous source of energy, excitement and enthusiasm.

Index

ABOUT THE AUTHOR

David Maister is widely acknowledged as one of the world's leading authorities on the management of professional service firms. For two decades he has advised firms around the world in a broad spectrum of professions, covering all strategic and managerial issues.

He is the author of the bestselling books *Managing the Professional Service Firm* (1993), *True Professionalism* (1997), and, with Charles H. Green and Robert M. Galford, *The Trusted Advisor* (2000).

In addition, he wrote or co-authored seven other books during his academic career, on such diverse subjects as truck drivers, managing an airline, and managing factory operations.

At least one of his books is available in Arabic, Dutch, French, Spanish, Indonesian, Japanese, Korean, Polish, Serbo-Croatian, and Chinese.

A native of Great Britain, David holds degrees from the University of Birmingham, the London School of Economics, and the Harvard Business School where he was a professor for seven years.

He lives in Boston, Massachusetts, and may be reached at:

Tel: 617-262-5968
Fax: 617-262-7907
e-mail: David_Maister@msn.com
Website: www.davidmaister.com